DR. R. A. VERNON'S
TEN RULES OF DATING

THE RULES HAVE CHANGED

Scripture Quotations

Unless otherwise indicated, all Scripture quotations are taken from the Holy Bible, New International Version®, NIV®. Copyright ©1973, 1983, 1984, 2011 by Biblica, Inc.™

Scripture quotations marked (NLT) are taken from the Holy Bible, New Living Translation, copyright ©1996, 2004, 2007, 2015 by Tyndale House Foundation.

Scripture quotations marked (MSG) are taken from The Message. Copyright ©1993, 1994, 1995, 2002, 2005, 2006 by Eugene H. Peterson.

Scripture quotations marked (ERV) are taken from the Holy Bible, Easy-to-Read Version™, copyright ©2006 by World Bible Translation Center, Inc.

Scripture quotations marked (GW) are taken from GOD'S WORD®, copyright ©1995 by God's Word to the Nations.

Scripture quotations marked (GNT) are taken from the Good News Translation® (Today's English Version, Second Edition) Copyright ©1992 by American Bible Society.

Scripture quotations marked (NASB) are taken from the New American Standard Bible®, Copyright ©1960, 1963, 1968, 1971, 1972, 1973, 1975, 1977, 1995 by The Lockman Foundation.

Scripture quotations marked (NRSV) are taken from the New Revised Standard Version Bible, copyright ©1989 by the Division of Christian Education of the National Council of the Churches of Christ in the USA.

Scripture quotations marked (CEV) are taken from the Contemporary English Version Copyright ©1995 by American Bible Society.

Scripture quotations marked (ESV) are taken from The Holy Bible, English Standard Version®, ESV®, copyright ©2001 by Crossway, a publishing ministry of Good News Publishers.

Scripture quotations marked (NKJV) are taken from the New King James Version®. Copyright ©1982 by Thomas Nelson.

All versions used by permission. All rights reserved.

CONTENTS

Part I: Laying the Foundation

Introduction To The Third Edition Of The Ten Rules Of Dating ... 1

The Three Types of Singles

- Single and Satisfied ... 13
- Single and Sinning ... 16
- Single and Seeking ... 20

Rule 1: You Must Have Self-Awareness ... 27

Rule 2: Know Your Non-Negotiables ... 61

Rule 3: Never Negotiate Your Non-Negotiables ... 82

Part II: Navigating the Dating Journey

Rule 4: Don't Play Date (Date on Assignment) ... 101

Rule 5: Have The Jesus Talk ... 114

CONTENTS

Rule 6: Know What Direction You're Dating In   138

Rule 7: Discuss Each Other's Pasts   162

Rule 8: Discuss Each Other's Present And Future Expectations   186

Part III: Preparing for Lasting Love

Rule 9: Hurry Up and Take Your Time   208

Rule 10: Don't Have Sex   229

INTRODUCTION TO THE THIRD EDITION OF THE TEN RULES OF DATING

You're holding a copy of my book in your hands, and yet, I can hear some of y'all asking: Another book on dating, Dr. Vernon? Really? After two already, what's left to say, and why now?

I'm glad you asked!

To answer your questions, *absolutely*, *plenty*, and from what I've seen and heard lately, *y'all still could use a little help*. I mean that with love. Let's take a look at a few of the hard facts that led me here.

- If you're single and in the market for love, ironically, you're not alone. According to the U.S. Census Bureau, over 46% of the U.S. population (just over 117 million people) are currently single, and about half of them are actively seeking a partner, using dating apps, going to social events, or asking their friends to hook them up.[1]

But finding love is not easy in today's world.

- Data from the Pew Research Center has found that 47% of Americans say dating is harder now than it was ten years ago, which is when I released the first edition of *Ten Rules*.[2]

- The Pew Research Center also found that two-thirds of people who are single and actively looking for a relationship say that their dating life is "not going too well" or "not well at all."[3]

- In the U.S. alone this year, online daters are expected to reach 35.5 million, but again, only half of them are looking for an exclusive romantic partner.[4]

- In a 2020 study, the majority of women said it's hard to find someone who is looking for the same kind of relationship and meets their standards.[5]
- In 2023, 45% of college-educated women cited an inability to find someone who meets their expectations as a major reason they are not dating, while only 28% of non-college-educated women felt the same.[6]

And there's more stats where those came from. These numbers paint a picture of a dating landscape that is challenging, confusing, and crowded. How do you find and keep lasting love in a world that is constantly changing, especially as a Christian who wants to honor God with your relationship? That's the question we're tackling in this book, one rule at a time.

I gave you the hard facts, now let me share some personal observations and reasons why a third edition of *Ten Rules* was needed.

REASON #1

Times have changed, and so has dating. The little black book my boys and I used to keep in our back pockets to collect numbers of girls we tried to holler at is now ancient history, as outdated as eight-track tapes and rotary telephones. Now, it all goes down in the DMs.

And remember when meeting someone online was taboo? *Hold up...* some of y'all may *not* remember because you were just kids then. Let me take you back real quick. In '95, only 2% of people met their partners on the web, as hooking up online was as shameful as being caught in white after Labor Day. Now? Both are the new normal. In fact, according to a 2019 study, the Internet is the number one way people link up, surpassing bars/restaurants, through friends, or at work or school.[7]

INTRODUCTION TO THE THIRD EDITION OF THE TEN RULES OF DATING

So, whether you're from the old school and remember the days before Tinder and TikTok or you're from the new school and all you've known is pinch and zoom, it makes no difference because today, we're all in the same class, where 'likes' and 'comments' can indicate attraction, and 'read receipts' are the new "I got your message."

But what's really wild is how rapidly the culture of courtship and dating protocols have shifted too. We've had to invent a whole new vocabulary to communicate and describe dating practices, from ghosting to orbiting, breadcrumbing to benching.

Have no idea what I'm talking about? Don't feel bad. I had to Google some of these terms myself. Let me define them for you.

Ghosting: When someone abruptly stops all communication with no explanation or goodbye. It's like they never existed. They don't respond to your texts, calls, or DMs and just seem to vanish into thin air.

Orbiting: When someone ghosts you but still keeps tabs on your social media accounts, liking and commenting on your posts as if nothing happened. It's like they're circling you from a distance, hence the term "orbiting."

Breadcrumbing: When someone gives you just enough attention to keep you hooked but never fully commits to anything. They might send flirty texts or make plans but always have an excuse for why they can't follow through. They're leaving "breadcrumbs" for you to follow.

Benching: Similar to breadcrumbing except the person has multiple potential partners on rotation and keeps you on the "bench" until they're ready to play (that is, commit).[8]

And these are just a few examples. I could go on and on with terms like *sneaky links, submarining, stashing,* and *cuffing*. Honestly, I don't even know how y'all single folk keep up. It's exhausting just listing these terms, let alone dealing with them firsthand. But that's the reality of dating these days—constantly navigating a minefield of Tinderellas and Tinderfellas giving mixed signals and ambiguous affection.

There was a time when people dated with the goal of finding a soulmate—someone to settle down with and build a future together. Now, people are happy with casual hookups and no-strings-attached situationships.

To some, the idea of building a life with one person sounds old-fashioned, unnecessary, or even boring, and the lines between friends and flings are as fuzzy as the filter-enhanced photos flooding our feeds.

Conventional courtship has been replaced by a throng of threads, communication reduced to a string of emojis, and authenticity buried beneath layers of digital deception.

With the rise of technology, our world is more connected than ever. But as we swipe through endless photo and video sharing dating apps and websites, it's clear that all this progress has come at a price. And in the economy of love in the age of algorithms, it seems like that price just keeps going up. The Internet has made finding prospects a breeze but vetting them a nightmare. It's a whole new world, and the more things change, the more they... get complicated.

Dating was tricky before the digital revolution. Now our brains, once wired for slow-burning love stories, are held hostage to the dopamine drip of endless scrolling. After the dopamine wears off, however, we're still craving the kind of nourishment only real relationship provides. Thanks to Zuck, Larry, and Sergey, we can feast on all the eye candy we want, but our souls are still starving. We think we want options but give us too many and we're indecisive, disappointed, and disillusioned. Scroll. Swipe. Sigh.

INTRODUCTION TO THE THIRD EDITION OF THE TEN RULES OF DATING

Life now moves at the speed of the double-tap, decisions are made in a snap, and ditching people is as easy as hitting 'delete.'

As a society, we're driven by a hunger for immediate satisfaction and endless stimulation. We have no patience for waiting, no discernment for choosing, and no depth for relating. We rush, we react, we regret. We are losing the virtues of patience, careful consideration, and deep connection.

Throw the pandemic in the mix and boom, we've got a shaken and stirred mocktail of uncertainty and loneliness with a splash of desperation. We had little choice but to adapt to the circumstances we found ourselves in. Even as we craved closeness, the coronavirus kept us apart, causing us, in many ways, to have to redefine what romance looked like.

And although the pandemic and its accompanying restrictions have receded for the most part, the 'ghost of COVID past' still looms, haunting our expectations, interactions, and hopes for meaningful relationships.

REASON #2

Technology and pandemic aside, the second and maybe greatest reason I have for writing this third edition is that the longer I stay married, the more I long for everyone to have what I have, to experience the love, lust, and longevity that I'm enjoying with my girl, my babies' mama, my wife, Victory.

At nearly thirty years in, I know that what we have is special, maybe even rare, based on the many conversations I've had with couples and colleagues who do not feel the same way about their spouses. What I consider my greatest blessing—the joy of my marriage—has created a burden in equal measure. As a Christian and as a pastor, I want as many people as possible to know the same level or, if it's possible, an even higher level of satisfaction, delight, and euphoria in their covenant commitments as I relish in mine.

It breaks my heart to see so many people struggle in their relationships or give up on finding true love altogether. I care deeply about dating because I care even more about marriage. And if you're a believer like me, you know that dating is not an end in itself, it's a means to an end, and that end is marriage. Marriage *is* the relationship goal. It's the ultimate expression of love, lifelong commitment, partnership, and friendship. Marriage is a good thing but more importantly, it's a God thing, which is why I'm so passionate about helping you make sure your dating life is too.

A QUICK DISCLAIMER

Now, before we go any further, I need to make something clear in case somehow you haven't already caught it. This book assumes your belief in God and a traditional or spiritual view of marriage, that is, one man and one woman. If you don't share that belief, this book may not be for you and getting married might not be the move.

Why? I just told you marriage is a God thing; *He* created it, not us. So, if you don't believe in Him, it's Kool & The Gang. I just don't want you to waste your time here. You're gonna hear me talk about God and marriage a lot and, are you ready for this? If you're not a believer, I think it's silly for you to get married. Seriously. I'm trying to free you.

If you don't rock with God, then presumably, His rules don't matter to you and you can do your thing without worrying about His consequences. Have as much sex as you want, with as many people as you want, in as many ways as you want. Date, hook up, break up, and move on as you please, because if there's no life after this, why not live however you want to live right now? With so many beautiful people on this planet, being with only one for the rest of your life is hardly natural; it's *super*natural. It's spiritual.

Which is why, for those of us who *do* believe in God, we can't get down like that. Well, technically we can, because we have free will, but we're held accountable to a Higher Power. We don't just live for the moment; we live for eternity. For us, marriage is so much more than a "piece of paper." We don't get to enter and exit as we please because it's not just a temporary deal, it's a permanent promise. We're committed for the long haul. In the words of Outkast, forever. *Forever ever? Forever ever.*

This covenant we agree to is non-negotiable. As believers, we have only three legit reasons to end a marriage: adultery, abuse, or abandonment. Anything else and we've got Matthew 19:9 hanging over our heads reminding us that divorcing and remarrying without biblical grounds is tantamount to adultery. Who wants that on their conscience? Not me, and I don't think you do either.

So yes, our standards are higher and our journey longer, but let me tell you something: Our rewards are greater too. All I'm trying to say here is, if God is not a part of your equation, then there are probably other books (and lifestyles) that make more sense for where you are. Still, my prayer is that through this work or otherwise, you do come to make Jesus your first love, and then find and fall in love with whoever He has for you.

LET'S TAKE A PAUSE FOR THE CAUSE

If you're still with me, picking up what I've been putting down, then that might've felt a bit heavy, so let me lighten things up a bit.

With the inherent selflessness and sacrifice that comes with following God's plan for marriage, I can understand why some people believe and promote the idea that God designed marriage to make us holy, not to make us happy. I get that perspective and it's a noble idea, but I disagree.

I believe He designed it for both.

I don't see God creating marriage as an incubator just to teach us to be more like Him. After all, there are countless ways He could train us in holiness and righteousness without binding us to another flawed human being in a lifelong commitment.

No, I think God wants us to revel in the rapture of love and shared companionship, a safe, sacred bond where we can find joy in each other's presence, crack up until our sides ache, and make love until we are breathless with delight. I mean, the Lord did invent both laughter and orgasms, did He not? And the latter, He created just for the marriage bed, might I add. For procreation too, but let's be real. He could have made that process a whole lot more clinical and dispassionate, and yet, He didn't. God wants us to enjoy the pleasure of marital ecstasy.

So, who says holiness can't go hand in hand with happiness? Why do the two have to be mutually exclusive? They don't. In my view, marriage brings both joy and character when God is at the center. It can be a beautiful blend of pleasure and purpose, challenge and ease, sacrifice and reward, shared intimacy as well as self-discovery.

I can say this with my chest because I'm living it every day. Twenty-six years in, I'm not guessing about anything when it comes to the possibilities of a godly marriage. Marriage is a container where we can become more like Christ *and* have a ball with our boo thang. Win-win.

From lovemaking to decision-making, from traveling across the country to spending staycations in bed, from blending our bloodlines to raising our babies, from the highs of seeing our grandchildren born to the lows of burying loved ones, Victory and I have weathered it all together. Through each wave and dip, every peak and valley, we've held fast to the unshakeable foundation of our faith—and to each other.

INTRODUCTION TO THE THIRD EDITION OF THE TEN RULES OF DATING

Apart from getting saved, the best thing I have ever done, by far, is choose her. She's the love of my life, my ride or die. I don't say this to brag. I say it because for those of you who want this life, I want you to find the love of your life too; for you to choose well, to marry right, to be with the person who will inspire you to become the best version of yourself. This is my raison d'etre.

You may be thinking, *Nobody's that in love. Is he for real? He must be capping.* I get this a lot. Even some of my close friends, colleagues, and fellow pastors doubt me. They wonder if anyone can be this happy in marriage, and to me, their skepticism is a sad indictment on the state of relationships today, a grim reminder that so many people have given up on the dream of experiencing love in its purest, most godly form—unconditional, lifelong, and fun. Yes, marriage can be fun. Marriage *is* fun.

I'm not fronting or faking. I'm living my best life with my best friend. And I'm here to tell you that it's possible for you too.

Don't get me wrong. My life is far from perfect, and I have struggles and scars. I have situations that are painful to think about, frustrations and disappointments, and areas of my life that would definitely be different if I had my way or say. Such is life. In my experience, you don't get it all.

You don't get to have a great marriage, and great parents, and great kids, and great everything. There's always something that leaves a hollow pang in your heart, a gap that you yearn to fill, or some strained relationship.

Life is a mixed bag, an unpredictable journey with glorious wonders and heart-wrenching tragedies. This is an inescapable existential reality, and it's why I believe God overcompensates us in some areas to account for where we've been shortchanged in another. Here's a truth you should remember:

Life is a delicate balance between the choices we make and the cards we are dealt. We may not have control over the hand we get, but we can control who we choose to play it with.

This choice can be one of the best decisions we ever make, or one of the worst, and I've seen both outcomes in my congregation, community, and even my own kin. It's why I'm so passionate about encouraging you to choose wisely, as this single choice will shape your entire life.

REASON #3

Simply put, the third reason I'm writing this book is because I've changed. My first book came to life when I was in my thirties. By my second book, I had hit my forties. Now, in my early fifties, my perspectives on many aspects of life, love, and faith have evolved. What I thought was absolute truth before, I now see with more clarity and nuance. The distance I've traveled, proverbially and literally, has taught me new lessons and imparted fresh revelation.

For over twenty years, I've been blessed with the privilege of walking alongside folks trying to figure this whole relationship thing out. I've stood by them through seasons of heartbreak and rejoiced with them in times of celebration. Through earnest discussions and candid confessions, my goal has always been to offer wisdom drawn from the well of my lived experience and distilled through God's word, will, and way.

In no way do I claim to be an expert in all things, but with thousands under my pastoral care and providing dating and marriage advice to leaders across secular and sacred realms, relationships are where I am at the top of my game and my expertise shines.

A NOTE ON THESE RULES

If you read my earlier works or listen to my teachings, some of these rules will sound familiar. But as life keeps teaching me, I plan to keep teaching you, so know that this book isn't just a rehash of old advice. It's a revised take on enduring principles, as well as expanded thinking on subjects I've covered before. There's also a good amount of new ground we'll tread together that resonates more with today's reality. A whole new generation has sprung up. With so many singles still wasting years and getting hurt out here, I want to help.

Whether you're loving the single life or struggling to find your person, this book is for you. It's tailored to people seeking to find and maintain lasting love, to those who want to date wisely and marry well, and to those who desire to honor God with their entire being.

These rules aren't just guidelines—they're lifelines, pulling you closer to the love you deserve. More than mere tips or tricks, they are principles and practices that will prepare you for one of the most important decisions of your life, second only to your salvation.

To be clear, this book is not a magic solution or a guarantee that you'll find a match made in Heaven, or frankly, any match at all. It won't solve all your dating problems, nor will it answer all your relationship questions. But it should help you date with purpose, intention, and clarity. If it points you in that direction and brings you closer to the love you desire and deserve, then I've done my job.

And now, I invite you to join me on this journey to discover the ten rules of dating that will change your life. Are you ready? Then keep reading and let's get up close and personal with the three types of singles.

THE THREE TYPES OF SINGLES

There are a lot of reasons why you might be single right now. Maybe you've gone through a breakup, a divorce, or you've lost someone you love. Perhaps you're in a season of singleness because you're recovering from or working through past trauma of some nature. All reasons are real and all are valid. But since you're reading this, I have a sneaky suspicion you're ready (or almost ready) to dip your toes back into the dating pool. Fortunately for you, you've come to the right place.

Regardless of how old you are, or what stage of life you're in; whether you're dating for the first time or dating again after a long time; have kids, grandkids, or no kids at all; this book is for every single soul out there, and that includes you.

While dating priorities often change as we get older—that hot and heavy romance you envisioned in your twenties may not be as high as your preference for long talks and long walks in your fifties—one thing remains constant: the human need for closeness, understanding, and love. This desire is universal, timeless, and God-given. I crafted these rules with this truth in mind, so rest assured that this advice applies to you wherever you are on your unique journey. And with that, let's get into these categories.

STAGES OF THE SINGLE LIFE

Through my research and counsel over the years, I've discovered that there are basically three kinds of singles: *single and satisfied, single and sinning*, and *single and seeking*.

INTRODUCTION TO THE THIRD EDITION OF THE TEN RULES OF DATING

SINGLE AND SATISFIED

These people are content in their singleness. They may be single by choice, having not found anyone who truly sparked their interests or because they are focused on their careers, spiritual growth, or other pursuits. These individuals are comfortable in their skin and at ease in the stage of life they are in, maximizing every opportunity to live a meaningful life without the demands of a romantic relationship.

They're not against companionship; they simply don't yearn for it like some do. Companionship to them may be a by-product of a life well lived, but it is not their ultimate goal.

Then there are other folk who are satisfied with being single because they have been played in love and refuse to put themselves in a position to have it happen again. Broken hearts, messy divorces, and bad relationships have left them with deep scars. These individuals, once bitten, twice shy, and often traumatized by past experiences, wear their independence like armor and claim to be content with being by themselves for the rest of their lives.

For those of you who've gotten burned and sworn off dating forever, I ask a simple question: Just because you had a few bad meals in your life, did you give up eating completely? Of course not. You simply found a better place to eat. The same goes for love. Just because you had some bad relationships doesn't mean you have to give up on finding a good one altogether.

If you truly are content being by yourself, that's great. There's nothing wrong with being happily single. In fact, the Bible even recommends it in certain cases.

"I Ain't Never Scared"

But let's face it, sometimes "satisfied" is just code for "scared." I've seen plenty of *supposedly* satisfied singles swiftly switch it up when the right one came along—that wall they'd built around their hearts came tumbling down faster than the wall of Jericho.

However, if trepidation is holding you back from finding the love you deserve, maybe it's time to give it another shot, to tap into that courage and take a chance on someone worthy of your time, energy, and effort. Don't let fear be the bouncer that blocks your entry to the club of companionship. You're worthy of love and you were born with the capacity to both give and receive an abundance of it. You may have some battle scars but those scars need not define you. Let them remind you that you survived but never let them limit your vision of what is possible.

Now, if you know you're not healthy enough to date, take all the time you need to heal, because the last thing you want to do is bring your baggage into a new relationship. Deal with your issues before you start something new. Then, once you've unpacked hurts that have been zipped up, sorted and separated truth from feelings, and aired out your emotions (with a therapist, not your ex), you can reopen your heart to the possibility of love.

Even then it won't be easy. You can't control what other people do or predict how your love life will turn out, but if you play by the rules that follow, you'll be way more ready to handle whatever comes your way.

A Biblical Example

The Apostle Paul was definitely about that single life.

He says in 1 Corinthians 7:8-9 (MSG):

> I do, though, tell the unmarried and widows that singleness might well be the best thing for them, as it has been for me. But if they can't manage their desires and emotions, they should by all means go ahead and get

married. The difficulties of marriage are preferable by far to a sexually tortured life as a single.

He continues in verses 32-35:

> I want you to live as free of complications as possible. When you're unmarried, you're free to concentrate on simply pleasing the Master. Marriage involves you in all the nuts and bolts of domestic life and in wanting to please your spouse, leading to so many more demands on your attention. The time and energy that married people spend on caring for and nurturing each other, the unmarried can spend in becoming whole and holy instruments of God. I'm trying to be helpful and make it as easy as possible for you, not make things harder. All I want is for you to be able to develop a way of life in which you can spend plenty of time together with the Master without a lot of distractions.

Paul was hardcore about serving God. Marriage, in his eyes, was a distraction, a detour from his divine mission. He saw his time and energy as tools for Christ, not for domesticity.

However, for most people, the desire to get married is just as valid a calling as ministry. Love and family are the makings of a meaningful life. The rewards, challenges, and companionship woven into these relationships bring a unique kind of fulfillment, a sense of belonging and completion that can't be replicated through other pursuits.

It's also important to consider the context of Paul's time. In Paul's day, marriage could seem like a waste of precious time that would be better spent saving souls because he thought Jesus' return was imminent. We, with the benefit of hindsight, know that Jesus didn't come back as soon as Paul thought He would.

So, what does this mean for you? If you're all about ministry, career goals, or spiritual growth, Paul's perspective might resonate with you. If you want to get married, however, feel free to embrace the treasures of love and partnership alongside your other goals and ventures.

SINGLE AND SINNING

If you're truly single and satisfied, then you don't want to be with anyone romantically or sexually. Period. But not everybody who dates sees single and satisfied this way, which brings me to the next group, *single and sinning*. Now these people might appear to be single and satisfied because they actually enjoy company and companionship, but they're in this category because they have no interest in commitment.

For them, it's all about the moment, the excitement of hooking up without the commitment of staying together. God and morality don't matter to them as they get into casual relationships, one-night stands, or friends with benefits situations. They're here for a good time, not a long time. They want the advantages that come with marriage, without the accountability. Typically, individuals who are content with this kind of existence don't even view their lifestyle as sinful, as faith and morality aren't central to their lives.

But 1 Corinthians 6:18-20 (GW) tells us that this isn't the way:

> [18] Stay away from sexual sins. Other sins that people commit don't affect their bodies the same way sexual sins do. People who sin sexually sin against their own bodies. [19] Don't you know that your body is a temple that belongs to the Holy Spirit? The Holy Spirit, whom you received from God, lives in you. You don't belong to yourselves. [20] You were bought for a price. So bring glory to God in the way you use your body.

The Bible clearly states sex out of wedlock is a sin and speaks strongly against it:

Ephesians 5:3 (NLT), "Let there be no sexual immorality, impurity, or greed among you. Such sins have no place among God's people."

Need more proof? 1 Thessalonians 4:3 (NLT) reads, "God's will is for you to be holy, so stay away from all sexual sin."

Notice the Bible says, "all sexual sin," which I believe includes sex with yourself. Sex is only pure when it occurs within the holy union of marriage. Period point blank. Indulging in pornography, self-pleasure, phone sex, or sleeping with someone you're not married to are all acts that are out of bounds for believers. God's design for sex is for it to flourish within the container and covenant of marriage. *Dassit.* I understand that this may sound old-fashioned or unpopular today, but holiness is still right. Can I get an amen?

It's Hard Out Here

Now, let me address the common arguments I hear. "Pastor," they'll say, "It's hard out here. I'm doing my best, but the temptation is real."

Believe me, I get it. I'm a pastor but I'm a man first, and I have eyes. I'm not immune to the appeal of beautiful women. But like Job, I've made a covenant with my eyes, and I honor it. It's a conscious decision to prioritize my relationship with God and my commitment to my wife.

Furthermore, temptation is not a sin. You can be tempted all day, and you're in bounds. Now, I wouldn't recommend consistently putting yourself in situations where you know you're going to have to rely on willpower and self-discipline, but it only becomes sin when you give in to whatever (or whomever) you're tempted by.

The Bible says that Jesus Himself was tempted in the wilderness (see Matthew 4). After fasting for forty days, to say he was hungry is probably an understatement. Satan knew Jesus was famished and tried to get Him to use his supernatural power to turn stones to bread.

But Jesus had the coldest response. He replied, "Man shall not live by bread alone, but by every word that proceeds out of the mouth of God." He saw through the trap, the seeds of doubt Satan was sowing about God's provision and the lure to disobey, and He didn't fall for it. He shut the devil down by countering with Scripture, staying focused and faithful.

When Temptation Has You Trippin', Tap Back Into Truth

First Corinthians 10:13 (NLT) says, "The temptations in your life are no different from what others experience. And God is faithful. He will not allow the temptation to be more than you can stand. When you are tempted, he will show you a way out so that you can endure."

This scripture right here is the one. It tells us that even in the face of strong desires, we're not helpless. There's always a way out. That's good news! The lesson here is that even in moments of vulnerability, we can resist temptation because we are equipped with the means to resist it.

Divine Hacks For Dodging Temptation

This may mean we have to avoid certain environments, change the company we kick it with, or be really careful with the kind of content we consume. But let's not even reduce resisting temptation to just avoiding what we shouldn't do, because it's also about spending time engaging in activities we should do.

Spend time involved in practices that nurture your mind, body, and spirit. When we put our focus here, we have less room to be tempted in the first place. Build relationships—non-romantic ones—with people who will hold you accountable to living a godly life. Not so they can be all in your business—I know you're grown—but so they can

INTRODUCTION TO THE THIRD EDITION OF THE TEN RULES OF DATING

look at you crazy when you do something crazy. They won't even have to say anything. A confused look from an observant friend is enough to plant the seeds of conviction and make you watch your step when you know you're acting in a way that doesn't align with who you said you want to be.

Also, when you start to get to know Jesus on a deeper level and draw closer to His purpose for you, sin will start losing its grip. Stay mindful of your weak spots so you can proactively guard your heart and mind when the enemy attacks. He's crafty and often strikes when you're most susceptible, but you have the power to protect your assignment and your anointing.

Single, Sinning, And Sabotaging: Borrowing Against Your Future Happiness

When you're single and sinning, you may be tempted to think, *I'm not hurting anyone.* But the truth is, there are at least two victims—future you and future bae. For your part, sin can lead to shame, guilt, co-dependence, and other terrible consequences. Further, do you not know that your body is the temple of the Holy Spirit, who is in you, whom you have received from God? You don't own you; you were bought at a price. These aren't my words. This is Bible, 1 Corinthians 6:19-20 to be exact. Your body is home to the Holy Spirit—you can't just have the Spirit on the 'Hot Mess Express' while you're getting it in on any given night.

As far as your future spouse, even before you meet him or her, every decision you make has the potential to impact them. Indulging in sexual sin can create unrealistic expectations, painful memories, and even comparisons that can dull the bliss and sanctity of your future marriage bed. All that time invested in flings is time stolen from your soulmate. It's unfair to them and to your future relationship to carry these extra layers of complexity into your shared life.

And hold up. I just thought about somebody else you're hurting—the one you're sinning with. Yeah, they're grown and responsible for their own choices, but you're not exempt from the role you play in them making the choice. You're not only accountable for your own actions, but also for the influence you have on others.

The enemy is gonna try it. Satan wants you to think you're missing out on something, that you're entitled to do whatever you want with your body, that God's rules are outdated and irrelevant. He's gonna hype you up with cheap thrills and callings of the flesh and then leave you hanging out to dry. Those quick fixes will leave you unfulfilled, searching for more of what can never satisfy.

The truth is, however, that God's rules are for your protection, not your restriction. He knows what's best for you, and He wants you to enjoy the gift of sex within its proper context, the boundaries of marriage. That's where you'll find the most pleasure, peace, passion, and purpose. Once you understand this, you'll go from single and *sinning* to single and *winning*.

If you do slip up and find yourself single and straying from the path, don't trip. Know that God offers redemption and grace to every prodigal. Ask for forgiveness, repent, and move on. The struggle is temporary; the reward is forever.

SINGLE AND SEEKING

And finally on our spectrum is *single and seeking*. These are people who are actively looking for a partner. They may be using dating apps, going to social events, or asking their friends to hook them up. They have a clear vision of what they want in a relationship, and they're not afraid to go after it. They're not playing games, nor are they wasting time. They're serious about finding love and they're willing to put in the work to make it happen.

INTRODUCTION TO THE THIRD EDITION OF THE TEN RULES OF DATING

If this is you, you're officially single and seeking. You're looking for love, and that's what's up. You're not needy or thirsty, you're just honest.

There's no shame in admitting you'd rather snuggle than struggle.

You know how God made you and it wasn't for the single life. You want to be married. You want to make love, maybe make some babies, and make a life with someone who complements your hustle. You want to serve God with them and get whatever goodness He has planned for the two of you as a couple. You want a soulmate, not a sidepiece. You're out here trying to build something real with someone who wants the same—a fun, faithful, forever love. And that's a beautiful thing.

In this case, you are officially seeking, and while seeking doesn't mean desperate, you want to stay mindful of your moods and movements so that your discernment doesn't devolve into desperation. Desperation repels. Discernment attracts. Allow me to explain.

When you're actively looking for a life partner, it's crucial to approach the process with a clear head and a grounded sense of self. You're not just casually dating or going with the flow (we'll unpack this more in Rule 4); you have a specific goal in mind—to find someone to build a meaningful, lasting relationship with, one that honors God and aligns with His purpose for your life.

But there's a fine line between seeking and desperation. Seeking is about being proactive and purposeful in your search for love. It's about knowing what you want and taking steps to find it, while still maintaining a healthy emotional balance. Desperation, on the other hand, is that sense of urgency, neediness, and even fear that can creep in when you're feeling the pressure to find "the one."

That's why it's so important to stay mindful of your moods and movements. Pay attention to your emotional state and your actions. Are you coming from a place of confidence, patience, and trust in God's timing? Or are you letting anxiety, impatience, or insecurity run the show?

When you're in a healthy seeking mindset, you're able to exercise discernment—the ability to see people and situations clearly, to make wise choices based on your values and goals. You're not just chasing after any potential partner; you're being selective and setting appropriate boundaries.

But when seeking turns into desperation? That's when things can get messy. Desperation can cloud your judgment big time. It can blind you to warning signs, compel you to lower your expectations, or cause you to accept less than what you're worth. You might find yourself grasping for any prospect of love, even if deep down you know it's not right for you.

Desperation pushes potential partners away. It can come across as clingy, needy, or even a little manipulative. On the flip side, discernment is straight-up attractive. When you're grounded in your own worth and clear about what you're looking for, you radiate an energy of authenticity and self-respect. You're not chasing after love or trying to force something to happen; you're simply open to the right opportunities and connections.

We all know people who go running heart-first into relationships like it's an emergency exit from loneliness, but let's face it; that's as effective as using a band-aid on a broken bone. You've heard me say it before and I'll say it again: It's better to be alone than married wrong. I have receipts to prove it.

Don't let the world lie to you and make you feel like you're not enough just because you're single. You don't need someone to stamp a

INTRODUCTION TO THE THIRD EDITION OF THE TEN RULES OF DATING

seal of validation on your worth or convert your loneliness into joy. This isn't possible anyway. Real joy is an inside job; it comes from knowing God and knowing who you are in Him. And let me remind you, He already loves you like crazy! Nothing can change that.

Can people make us happy? Of course they can. A smile, a compliment, a gift, an appreciation post—these are all things people can do to make us happy. But can they keep us happy? Nah. Because these same people can also side-eye, criticize, "cancel," and blast us, and then it's just us and our decision to put them on a pedestal where they did not belong in the first place.

Lauryn Hill said it best in her song "Superstar" when she pointed to Jesus Christ as proof of this fact:

> *They'll hail you then nail you,*
> *No matter who you are.*
> *They'll make you now then take you down...*

Ain't that the truth? Folk are quick to lift you up when you're riding high, but the moment you stumble, they're just as quick to tear you down. It's a harsh reality, but it's one we have to face head-on.

People are flawed, so if your expectation is for your relationships, romantic or otherwise, to be a seamless source of happiness, then you've got it twisted because humans are gonna human, and when they do, you're gonna be disappointed. Basing your happiness on people who are flaky by nature is a raw deal.

I know the longing for that special someone can feel heavy. Like you're missing out on the relationship you want so badly. But worrying about it won't make a mate magically appear, so shift that energy into areas you can control. And please don't settle just to say you've got somebody. Let God surprise you instead of trying to force things to happen. The timeline for when that special someone will walk into your life is above you now, so you have to just trust that it's unfolding perfectly. Live fully while praying boldly and believe that whoever and whatever God has destined for you is already on the way.

Come Correct Before You Connect

Now, since you're seeking, let me just give you this right now: The best way to enter a relationship is to bring your whole self to the table, not a half-empty plate, talking about you're looking for somebody to complete you. Only the Most High can do that, beloved, and if you're a believer, it's already done (Colossians 2:10).

> **You've got to be a whole meal by yourself before you can even think about cooking something up with someone else.**

The truth is, you attract who you are, not just who you want, so if you're not whole, do you really expect to pull someone who is? Come with your cup overflowing with self-love already. Have your own sense of identity and purpose before pursuing partnership. Be content in your own company and so aware of your worth that you'd rather roll solo than settle.

Know who you are, what you want, and don't allow a person looking for you to complete them to sweep you off your feet either, because two halves don't make a whole when it comes to a relationship. It just makes for a fractured relationship.

> **You and your potential mate have to both be good single before you can be great together.**

INTRODUCTION TO THE THIRD EDITION OF THE TEN RULES OF DATING

So, learn to be cool by yourself. The perks of singleness are plentiful. It's a time to invest in yourself, develop your interests and passions, and to cultivate a strong sense of self. Being at ease with who you are and finding happiness in solitude sets the stage for attracting and maintaining a meaningful connection with someone else.

At the same time, what we're not gonna do is downplay the significant and beautiful role a partner can play in your life in the name of being single and winning. While it's crucial to find fulfillment and happiness within yourself, it's also important to recognize that the right relationship can bring immense joy, support, and growth to your life.

When you connect with the right person, it *will* change your entire life. If you're good before you get married, just wait till you see what happens once you join your life with the person you're meant to be with.

For example, if you're someone who wants to conquer the world, as it were, the right man or woman will make you feel like you're already on top of it. With them by your side, no challenge seems too great to overcome. You'll feel lighter in their presence, as if they lift weight off your shoulders. When you find the one who fits into every part of you and who gets you like no other, you'll be in a position to appreciate them in a way you simply cannot if you're not already whole.

Keep in mind, whole doesn't mean perfect. But as long as you remember that your partner is not in your life to fix you, nor are they the source of your happiness or validation and vice versa, you won't have the pressure of these unrealistic and unfair expectations getting in the way of your ability to connect. Your future spouse is the icing on the cake, not the cake itself. They should enhance your life, not define it.

Before We Move On

If you're single and seeking, one other thing you'll want to be crystal clear about is the intention of the person you choose to date. You want to make sure he or she is also single and seeking, that they want what you want, a real, meaningful relationship. Don't choose any ol' body who isn't choosing you back. There are plenty of folks out here wasting people's time and playing games. You come as a full course, but they treat you like a snack.

Ladies, listen up. If a man says he's looking for a wife but his actions are sketchy, pay attention to the signs: Is he inconsistent in communication, taking days to text back but claiming he loves to talk to you? Does he make excuses to avoid introducing you to his close friends and family? Does he keep you separate from key areas of his life instead of integrating you?

If so, something isn't adding up. Watch his moves, not just his mouth. Sweet talk can distract you from real intentions. Believe what you see.

Fellas, same for you. If she says she's ready to settle down but shies away from commitment conversations, gets weird when you bring up the future, and avoids introducing you to the main people in her life, she may not be ready for that long-term love even if she looks and sounds the part. Watch for inconsistencies.

Nobody's perfect, but patterns are telling. Your potential match should be giving green lights, not red flags. Their words and their actions need to line up before you commit.

And with that, let's get into **Rule 1 | You Must Have Self-Awareness.**

RULE 1
YOU MUST HAVE SELF-AWARENESS

"Know thyself." -*Socrates*

Mirror, Mirror On The Wall: Who's The Most Deluded Of Them All?

So, you think you've got yourself all figured out, huh? Well, you might want to think again. Extensive research indicates we're not nearly as self-aware as we like to believe.

Turns out, a staggering 95% of us strut around fully convinced that we know ourselves, but the data says otherwise. A 2018 study published in the Harvard Business Review found that only 10-15% of people possess a strong sense of self-awareness.[9] Let that sink in. This means almost all of us are walking around in a fog of self-delusion and it begs the question: Are you in that number? Can you confidently say you are clear on what your desires, motivations, and needs are? Maybe you can, but maybe you shouldn't. At least not yet, because there's a good chance you're wrong.

I was shocked when I saw this statistic, but if it's true, it explains why so many singles have trouble finding meaningful and lasting relationships or misjudging what they really seek in a partner. Let's be honest, how many of us have entered the dating scene thinking we knew what we wanted, only to discover that maybe, just maybe, we weren't as ready as we thought?

Maybe you're still in this situation. You have a vague idea of your ideal partner but you haven't taken the time to truly introspect and define what you're looking for, so it's more like playing a game of pin the tail on the donkey. You might get what you want, but it'll be by random chance rather than deliberate choice. You might also end up feeling like somebody made a donkey out of you.

This revelation about how few people are self-aware was a game-changer for me. I took it as a clear sign that singles need a recalibrated approach to dating, beginning with self-reflection. It also confirmed that changing the first rule in this edition of the book to **You Must Have Self-Awareness**, was the right choice.

A Mission You Can't Refuse

This rule then, isn't just some fluffy advice or a casual suggestion. It is now your mission, and I must forewarn you, should you choose to accept it, this assignment is no small task. I'm going to walk you through it, but it will be intense and personal.

The journey of self-discovery is a daunting call to investigate the complex, contradictory mess of thoughts, feelings, and experiences that compose your inner world, and this chapter is your guide to getting to the heart of who you are. You're solving a mystery, where you're both the detective *and* the mystery.

You'll have to question your assumptions, audit your motivations, and dismantle your defenses. Your introspective methodology must include radical honesty, relentless curiosity, and the courage to confront uncomfortable truths.

You must also turn your attention outward to seek the perspectives of others. External perspectives provide an invaluable reality check against your subjective perceptions, reflecting aspects of yourself that you might not otherwise see.

The Paradox Of Getting Older: Check Yourself Before You Wreck Yourself

Seeking external feedback is especially important for my mature readers. You have to be particularly vigilant about not assuming that because you have a lifetime of tales to tell, your viewpoints are beyond scrutiny or evolution. You may have "heard and seen it all before," but this is the very thing that puts you in a high-risk category for stubbornness, fixed perspectives, and an inflated sense of self-importance.

You can convince yourself that the outlook you've internalized over the years is totally right and complete, but beware of the illusion (or perhaps more precisely, *delusion*) that age has dispelled the ignorance of youth and thus, rendered you immune to blind spots. On the contrary, it has merely replaced old ones with new ones. This is just the kind of arrogance that causes many of us to cling to beliefs about ourselves that are no longer relevant or helpful for who and where we are today.

> **Experience can breed both wisdom and bias in equal measure. Be careful not to confuse or conflate the two.**

When it comes to self-awareness, age ain't nothing but a number. Every stage of life brings new challenges and changes that make self-discovery a lifelong process. Your younger, less experienced self may have taught you about ambition, spontaneity, and resilience, but your older self may need to learn new lessons about adaptability, humility, and the importance of patience, wisdom, and the art of letting go.

To keep your beliefs from calcifying into bias, you've got to hold your assumptions up to the light regularly, looking closely and critically so that you don't become cocky and satisfied with false certainty. Your experience should be a variable in your quest for continual self-understanding, but not a control that corners you into a fixed, flat way of thinking.

The Perilous Journey Most Won't Take—But You Will

You're probably starting to see that the path to self-knowledge is long, winding, and littered with blind spots. It's rugged and unforgiving at times. It diverges, doubles back, and is sometimes fraught with unexpected dead ends that force you to retrace your steps and return to where you started. At any given time, you may not even know where you are on the map.

When you consider how difficult it is to navigate the path to self-knowledge, is it really a surprise that only 10-15% of people are self-aware? With so many obstacles standing between us and genuine self-understanding, in addition to all the existential factors influencing our choices and behaviors, it's no wonder that dating can be such a confusing and frustrating experience.

I know, I know—this is a lot, but I warned you that there would be some heavy lifting on this mission. I can almost hear you saying, "Pastor, what kind of dating book is this? I thought you were gonna help me in my search for my soulmate, not expect me to do some soul searching!"

YOU MUST HAVE SELF-AWARENESS

Know Thyself, Find Thy Match

I get it. I really do. But what if I told you this journey of self-searching is not separate from your search for a soulmate, but rather, it's the pivotal first step? Consider what the Bible says in Matthew 7:7 (NIV), "... Seek, and you will find. So, taking for granted that you already found Christ, what do you think you should seek first: a partner, or an understanding of yourself? You have to sift through the layers of who you *think* you are to uncover who you *truly* are to date with clarity and sound judgment.

Rushing into romance without knowing yourself is how people end up married to strangers, weirdos, and dummies. Now *that's* work! If you want to find the right person, you must first become the right person and that starts with truly knowing who you are and what you want in a partner and in life.

I've got good news for you, however. Are you ready for your first shout? (*You do know I'm a preacher, right?*) By the time you finish these next three chapters, wrestle with the deep questions, and get your hands dirty digging through the soil of self-reflection, you are going to be in that number! And no, I'm not talking about when the saints go marching in. I'm talking about the 10-15% who did the work and got the wisdom. Becoming part of that self-aware minority means awakening to the richness and complexity of your own being, which is not just an achievement, it's a necessity.

This is where I come in as your guide. While I can't provide a warranty for your work—the only guarantee we have in love is that God's never fails—here's what I can promise you:

If you commit to the necessary work of self-awareness now, it will spare you countless headaches, heartaches, and hassles later.

I'm here to offer you heartfelt wisdom gleaned from a lifetime of navigating my own relationships, counseling others through theirs, and learning from the ultimate relationship expert, Jesus. I can also assure you that if you embrace this process, you will come through stronger, wiser, and more prepared for whatever love has in store for you. The journey won't be easy (nothing worthwhile ever is), but you will get stronger, so believe me when I tell you, the juice is worth the squeeze.

And speaking of juice, when the conscious poet and lyrical prophet Tupac Shakur dropped these lines...

> *Keep ya head up,*
> *Ooh, child, things are gonna get easier.*
> *Keep-keep ya head up, ooh, child, things'll get brighter (ohh).*

...he wasn't just spitting bars. He was preaching a sermon. Things will get brighter if you persevere.

God's Got Your Back
(And Your Front, And Your Sides)

This work *is* heavy, but it's holy. And it's in this blessed space of learning and knowing who and whose you are that you realize you're not in the work alone. Philippians 1:6 (NIV) tells us that "...He who began a good work in you will carry it on to completion until the day of Christ Jesus."

These words are a direct reminder that God is working too, and He is invested in your growth and transformation. He's not halfway in, He's all in. Even better, He signed up for the job knowing full well your shortcomings, your hang-ups, your faults, failures, flaws and all.

As we embark on this journey of self-awareness, particularly in the context of dating and relationships, bear in mind that the goal is to shed the old and welcome the new, to confront the shadows, so you can bask in the light.

By "old," I mean the outdated beliefs, bad habits, and stale mindsets that limit your potential and relationship satisfaction. These could be negative thought patterns, harmful narratives about yourself, or unhealthy relationship dynamics.

When I say "new," I'm referring to the fresh perspectives, constructive behaviors, and evolved mindset that emerges as you courageously examine cognitive constraints and replace them with self-awareness and more productive ways of seeing.

Shedding the old and embracing the new is like gardening. As you pull out the weeds of unhelpful habits and plant seeds for healthier ones, you'll start to notice changes. The soil of your life becomes fertile ground for relationships that thrive, and just like that, you're no longer chasing love, but growing it.

The "shadows" are the unexamined parts of your personality or the uncomfortable truths that you might shy away from confronting—the fears, insecurities, or unresolved past traumas that hinder your progress. In this freshly tended garden, however, you'll no longer feel the need to hide in shadows among the trees. You'll stand in the light, where everything that sprouts up is nurtured by self-knowledge and self-acceptance.

It's here that you not only find the insights you need to position yourself for the partner you desire, but you realize that love, in its truest form, starts within you. When you embrace this process in tandem with God's vision for your life, the hike from confusion to clarity and from heartache to healing, isn't just possible—it's promised.

The Dangers Of Dating Before Self-Discovery

Alright, so we've checked off some pretty big boxes. We have:

- ☑ Realized that we are not the self-aware gurus we thought we were.
- ☑ Figured out that getting to know ourselves is hard work.
- ☑ Grasped that the self-searching process is not separate from but central to our search for a soulmate.
- ☑ Learned that the road to self-discovery never really ends.
- ☑ Discovered that to stand in the light we have to leave the shadows.
- ☑ Understood that our walk with God is a key part of this whole equation.

Given these insights, it's time to tackle why jumping into the dating pool without a firm grasp of self is like doing a belly flop in the shallow end. It's the emotional equivalent of a blind leap. As you dive headfirst into murky waters, you might collide with something you can't see from the surface, like another person's unresolved issues. Or you could get caught in the dangerous riptide of mismatched expectations that eventually pull you under, away from your authentic self.

Just as a swimmer gauges the depth and current of a body of water before taking the plunge, you need to understand the depth and current of your own existence. When we skip this critical self-analysis step, we risk losing ourselves in another person or worse, drowning in their drama.

So, before we venture further into the practicalities of self-awareness, let me ask you: On a scale of 1-10, with 1 being "Who am I, even?" and 10 being "I'm my own soulmate," how well do you think you know yourself? How in tune are you with the core values that define you, the experiences that trigger you, the beliefs that drive you, and the passions that motivate you? Do you know your own personality so well that you can easily identify who you'll click with and who you'll clash with? Do you know exactly what you want and need in a relationship? Are your boundaries clearly defined?

If you answered yes to these questions, then you're crushing it. (*Why are you reading this book again? I'm kidding. There's much to gain here even if you are already living your best life as a single.*) If you answered no, then I've got good news: you're right where you're supposed to be, and by the time you finish reading this book, you'll have both a stronger sense of self and a clearer picture of what you're actually looking for.

Ignorance Is Not Bliss: The High Cost Of Low Self-Awareness

It's pretty clear that if you don't have a good handle on your inner workings, you'll pay a hefty toll in the currency of broken relationships. When you don't know yourself, you're more likely to hook up with someone based on convenience rather than compatibility, prioritizing the hunt for the ideal partner over an inward journey. The outcome, sadly, is as predictable as it is painful. Frequently, you'll find yourself trapped in relationships that are emotionally unsatisfying, spiritually stunted, or simply joyless. It's where the right person turns out to be the wrong person in the right disguise.

By not recognizing your own worth or understanding your core needs, you will shortchange yourself and compromise on needs you didn't even know you had. You'll pour time, energy, and resources into people you were never meant to date, let alone marry. Meanwhile, you'll inadvertently deprive both yourself and your partner of the fulfilling relationships you might have found, had you taken the time to understand yourself first.

When Self-UnAwareness Hits Home

Perhaps you've been in a relationship with someone who didn't know themselves and it didn't work out. Your partner may have grappled with their identity, causing them to vacillate between neediness and dominance. Maybe they cloaked their insecurities in passive-aggressive behavior, or they were just generally difficult in a way that kept you perpetually on edge, so you were constantly walking on eggshells around them, never able to truly be yourself.

Or maybe, despite your efforts to be the best man or woman you could be, it seemed you could never quite hit the target because your partner was always looking for something more. More attention, more affection, more validation—nothing ever seemed to be enough. When they ultimately moved on or were unfaithful, chasing a mirage of satisfaction elsewhere, all your efforts seemed to be in vain.

You were left feeling like a failure and you may have even held yourself responsible, thinking that if only you had been more patient, or more understanding, or more of whatever it was they seemed to be craving, then perhaps things would have been different. But let me free you: it was never about you. Their insatiable hunger for more was a manifestation of their own self-ignorance, as they were likely fighting their own battle of self-unawareness, a war internal and invisible.

If You Can't Say "Amen," Say, "Ouch"

Alternatively, you might be reading this book right now because *you* were the person who lacked self-insight and made all the wrong choices. You were the one always seeking more, trying to fill a void that you didn't understand, using relationships as a cover-up for your inner wounds. You were the one looking for something in your partner that you needed to find within yourself and who walked away from something good because you couldn't recognize its value at the time. *Ouch.* If this is you, there's no need for self-condemnation. In fact, this realization is a key step towards healing and self-discovery.

Why We Struggle With Self-Awareness

So why do we do this? Why do we enter the dating world with such little self-awareness? There are a few reasons:

1. **We're not taught how to cultivate self-awareness.** Most school curriculums don't include courses on self-discovery or emotional intelligence. Our parents may have given us some insight into who we are, but most likely not to the extent that will help us navigate dating and relationships.

2. **We're afraid to look inward.** Self-discovery can be uncomfortable. It means facing our flaws and insecurities head on. It requires vulnerability and honesty with ourselves, which can be scary.

3. **We want to fit in and be liked.** We often prioritize being accepted by others over understanding ourselves. This can lead us to suppress our own desires and personality traits, and instead adopt behaviors that we think others will find more appealing. In the process, we lose touch with who we truly are.

4. **We think we already know ourselves.** We live with ourselves every day so it's easy to assume we know everything there is to know about ourselves. But as we've discussed, true self-awareness takes work and it's an ongoing process.

As a result of these factors, many people don't take the time to get to know themselves before they start dating. This is why the first rule of dating is you must have self-awareness. Otherwise, you are bound to make the same mistakes over and over again, expecting a different result each time, which by definition, is insanity.

Self-Awareness Defined And Unpacked

Self-awareness is the ability to understand yourself, your emotions, your strengths, your weaknesses, your preferences, your personality, and your purpose. It is being attuned to the contours of your inner world—your thoughts, feelings, values, desires. It involves being acutely mindful of your quirks and idiosyncrasies, your emotional responses and reactions, behavioral patterns, stories, and ways of processing.

To be self-aware requires regularly examining your blind spots—the parts of yourself you tend to ignore, neglect, or deny—with curiosity and compassion. It's the ability to tell it like it is when you're talking to yourself and being brave enough to embrace the uncomfortable truths.

When you know yourself, you recognize what fuels your fire versus what extinguishes your spark. Self-awareness reveals which mindsets propel you forward and which ones paralyze your progress. It alerts you to your purpose; that drive that gets you out of bed every morning, ready to take on the day. Conversely, it also reveals your poison, the mindset that tempts you to pull the covers back over your head in defeat.

This self-knowledge gifts you with a strong sense of self-worth with goals that guide your actions, which is key to your overall station and satisfaction in life, as self-awareness blossoms into self-acceptance, self-confidence, and self-respect. It's also the key to finding someone who's compatible with you, who complements, challenges, and supports you, and who loves you for who you are.

Without self-awareness, how can you truly know what you want or need in a relationship? How can you set healthy boundaries or clearly communicate your desires to a partner if you haven't figured that out for yourself? When you aren't self-aware, you essentially enter relationships blind and mute, unable to spot red flags or articulate when your needs aren't being met. That's a dangerous place to be.

YOU MUST HAVE SELF-AWARENESS

But self-awareness is not only about looking inward, it's also about looking outward and being conscious of how others view you. (Remember those external perspectives we talked about earlier?) If there's a disconnect between how you see yourself and how a potential or actual partner sees you, cue the unnecessary drama because it's bound to show up.

For example, if you view yourself as easy-going but your partner sees you as indecisive, it can cause friction. They may interpret your laid-back nature as a lack of opinion or direction, which can lead them to assume you're disinterested or indifferent. Meanwhile, you're left feeling misunderstood and frustrated because you're only trying to keep the peace. Somewhere in translation, a signal is being scrambled and this will lead to discord and distance.

On the flip side, when you understand how others perceive you, you can deal with potential misunderstandings before they spiral out of control. You can have a conversation with your partner about how your calm demeanor is not a sign of indifference or lack of direction, but your way of avoiding unnecessary battles and evidence of how much you trust their judgment. That's the power of self-awareness. Know yourself and you'll know the qualities you need in a partner to cultivate a dynamic of open communication and deep connection.

Have self-clarity and your absolutes become unmistakable.

When you're self-aware, you won't compromise your core needs just to keep someone around because your boundaries are solid. You'll approach relationships with a sense of purpose and direction because you have a clear understanding of what you need in a relationship to feel valued, respected, and loved.

Without self-awareness, however, you'll lower your standards and unsure of what you need, grasp at false fulfillment. In other words, you'll start to negotiate your non-negotiables. (More on that in Rule 3).

How To Develop Self-Awareness

So, how do you cultivate this self-awareness? I'm glad you asked, but before we get to that, I want to point out that the younger you are, the more growth you've got ahead. Between the stages of adolescence and young adulthood, your physical development might progress rapidly, while your mental and emotional development take their sweet time catching up. This disparity can often lead to a tumultuous journey towards self-awareness.

Consider this: What happens when I'm a male in my mid-twenties and at my sexual peak, but I am not as emotionally mature or even conscious of the fact that I need to be thinking about what I truly need in a relationship?

Or, as a female, what if my breasts and behind are developed, but I don't yet have the well of life experiences to draw from that would help me truly understand my worth beyond physical appearance? My body seems ready for a relationship, but how do I know if my heart is?

This stage of life can feel like being handed the keys to a car before you've learned to drive. Sure, you can turn the engine on, but can you navigate the busy streets, maneuver around potholes, or know when to hit the brakes? This is where the rubber meets the road.

How do you determine if you're ready for a relationship then? The same way you determine if a seed is ready to sprout, which is kind of difficult to do because the reality is, you can't always see what's going on underneath the surface. It's not just about the readiness of the soil, but also the quality of the seed itself. Is it healthy? Does it have enough nutrients? What about the environment around it? Is there enough sunlight? Too much rain or not enough?

YOU MUST HAVE SELF-AWARENESS

Similarly, in determining your readiness for a relationship, you have to look below the surface at the hidden factors. It's not just your visible maturity that matters, but also your character and stability. Are you emotionally prepared and mentally resilient? Are you self-secure enough not to be dependent on others for validation? Do you have a spiritual core that keeps you grounded in times of adversity? Here's a big one: Do you feel ready to get married? Because if you're not ready to entertain the idea of a lifelong commitment, you shouldn't be dating.

If you'd been born a couple thousand years ago, you wouldn't even have to worry about dating because back then, marriages were arranged. Now, before you say arranging marriages is crazy, the divorce rate of arranged marriages in some cultures is as low as four percent.[10] I'm not suggesting that your parents pick your spouse, but if you have parents whom you trust, why not ask their opinion about the person you're thinking about spending the rest of your life with? My wife and I have helped two of our adult children pick well, and they're married and happy. We were able to offer them perspectives on certain aspects that they couldn't see clearly and guide them through the complexities of romance.

If seeking your parents' wisdom is an option, take it. But whether it is or isn't, the best thing you can do right now is apply the ancient, timeless, always on point sagacity of Proverbs 4:23 (NIV): "Above all else, guard your heart, for everything you do flows from it." This isn't just a cautionary statement; it's a strategic plan for self-preservation and intentional growth. Be extra cautious about who you let into your inner world and pray for wisdom beyond your years.

Similarly, Proverbs 3:5-6 (NIV) is a major key for all the decisions you'll ever have to make, including the ones you'll make about relationships. It says, "Trust in the Lord with all your heart and lean not on your own understanding; in all your ways submit to him, and he will make your paths straight."

Inexperience puts us at a disadvantage. Youth puts us at an even greater one. In dating, this makes for a risky combination. When your hormones are having a party, it's hard to tell fleeting attraction from lasting compatibility. Trying to figure out if you're into someone just because they're cute or because you genuinely click on deeper levels is equally challenging because making this distinction might require maturity you don't yet possess.

This is where godly insight becomes absolutely essential and where you have to fight to become as self-aware as possible in every facet of your life. Trust me when I tell you, your instincts alone won't cut it.

I've been in the trenches with couples who took the plunge into matrimony while still callow in their self-knowledge, young lovers who said "I do" before they really knew who 'I' even was. Fast forward twenty years, and they're living with a stranger, or worse, an enemy. They've both changed, matured, and discovered new passions and interests that pulled them away from and pitted them against each other, rather than bringing them closer together.

They overlooked (or were oblivious to) the cornerstone of compatibility, and now, the distance between them is more than just emotional—it's physical, with separate living spaces cementing their division. It's heartrending to witness, and it's the exact scenario I hope to help you avoid.

So, what's the key? How can you maximize your self-awareness as you search for love, regardless of your age or stage in life? Can you truly cut through life's clutter, get to know yourself, and understand what you need in a partner, while keeping God at the center of it all?

You bet you can. There's a whole lot you can do right now, to not only increase your self-awareness, but your discernment and spiritual insight too.

ENHANCE YOUR SELF-AWARENESS WITH THESE FOUR PRACTICES

Practice #1: Get Right With God

If you're looking to truly understand yourself, you've got to start with praying and seeking God. I know this seems like the obvious, predictable, easy answer, but that's because there is no better way to cultivate self-awareness than to engage in a daily dialogue with the One who created you.

God knows you inside out. He's seen your past, knows your present, and has planned your future. What better place to gain insight about your life than from the Source of all life? Why not get answers straight from the One who knows everything, including what's best for you? He knows exactly what you need, and what you want even more than you do. You know what you *think* you want; He knows what you *actually* want.

Start by having raw, candid conversations with Him. And if you want to know what I mean by raw, check out some of David's psalms. That brother did not hold back. He was the original straight shooter, laying out his sins, doubts, and regrets before God with no filter. And guess what? God didn't strike him dead for his honesty; on the contrary, He called him a man after his own heart.

So, do like David did and lay it all out in prayer—your hopes, fears, dreams, uncertainties. Don't hold back. God can handle your ugly cry. Ask Him to reveal the true you to you, the authentic, the raw, the uncut. Ask Him to help you have the courage to be honest and clear about who you are, where you are, and what it is you need to be doing in this season of your life. Pray for the strength to stay true to yourself and your path.

Be a good listener too. God speaks in different ways—through His word, people, synchronous situations, and that still, small voice inside you. Keep your ears and heart open, and when He affirms who you are and the plans He's got for you, take notes. Peep how He may correct your perspective or shift your focus away from what the world says to what He says. Don't sleep on His advice, don't shrug off His guidance.

Let God chisel away areas that need refining. Remember, He's the Potter, and we're just the clay (Isaiah 64:8). Instead of dictating to the Potter how you should be shaped, yield yourself to His capable hands. He's the one with the master plan, so when He moves, you move. Lean into His timing, His ways, His promises—His plans are not designed to disappoint.

When you keep in step with God by conversing with Him daily, you're signing up for blessings on blessings. He's got epic experiences tailor-made for your journey. So make praying and seeking God your top priority. He's not just the gateway to self-awareness; He's the plug for everything you need.

Practice #2: Reflect And Journal

After seeking God in prayer, another powerful way to cultivate self-awareness is through reflection and journaling.

Reflection is critical thinking about yourself, your life, experiences, feelings, relationships, thoughts, beliefs, values, goals, flaws, doubts, dreams, and fears without judgment.

Journaling is writing down these reflections to capture revelations, track personal growth, and gain self-awareness over time. There's a place for scribbling about what you ate for lunch and who got on your nerves today—but this ain't it.

When you combine these two practices, you get reflective journaling.

YOU MUST HAVE SELF-AWARENESS

Think of reflective journaling as a hand-to-heart conversation with yourself.

You are time traveling into your own psyche, giving voice to all versions of yourself, past, present, and potential. Through journaling, patterns become visible, insights surface, and with each entry, the aperture through which you see yourself broadens.

This practice of self-reflection and journaling is a formidable ally in your pursuit of self-awareness. It takes guts to face your own story head-on, to both call yourself out and cheer yourself on. But it's here, in the unguarded honesty of your own written words, that you'll find no greater confidant.

My suggestion? Carve out a few minutes each day for this practice. If that's too much of an ask, weekly or monthly check-ins can still serve you well. Find a time that fits your flow, a chill spot for contemplation, and choose the tool that feels right—be it the classic pen and paper, a digital document, or a voice recording. The medium can vary, but the mission remains the same: to give voice to your inner narrative.

The most profound self-discovery happens in stillness so to get you started on your journaling journey, I've curated a collection of prompts designed to provoke both thought and emotion. Give yourself the gift of quiet time to marinate on these. They're not for rapid-fire answering; they're for simmering on the back burner of your mind. Expect epiphanies as you unpack core aspects of your identity.

Because of the nature of these questions, I don't recommend you try to answer them daily, or even weekly. Do set a reminder to revisit them at least quarterly, as well as during major life milestones or transitions, and at the end of every year—you'll be amazed by your transformation over time. Plus, coming back to these reflections regularly keeps your self-knowledge fresh.

Some of your responses might surprise you, others might unsettle you. But all of them will broaden your understanding of your inner topography. If you give yourself the space to vent, grieve, rejoice, heal, process, analyze, clarify, prioritize, externalize, and strategize, the answers you provide will help you map your interior life, and stuff that has never made sense to you will start to stand out in your mind as if it's been hiding in plain sight the whole time.

So, when you're answering these questions, don't play yourself by sugar-coating your thoughts or rationalizing your feelings. Bring your full humanity to the page—confusion, complexities, hypocrisies, and all. You're not trying to impress anyone; you're trying to press into yourself.

And the best part is that it's in this intimate, innermost sanctuary of self-authoring where you get to meet God in a fresh and profound way. Show up for this work and watch Him do His.

Inward Bound: Journaling Prompts For Self-Exploration

These prompts are an invitation to pause, ponder, and peer into the recesses of your heart and mind. Listen to your life—it's speaking, and then write the story that only you can. Your experiences hold wisdom. Uncover your truest self by answering these questions. Let them guide you to greater self-awareness.

The Real Tea On Me

1. **Authenticity Audit:** When do you feel like you can be your absolute, unfiltered self? Describe that free-spirited you and the situations that bring out that version of you.

2. **Quality Reassurance:** What qualities within yourself do you feel proud of, and which do you want to improve? Explore the reasons behind these feelings.

3. **Counting Blessings:** Right now, what aspects of your life fill you with gratitude, and how do these areas impact your overall well-being?

4. **Outside Perspectives:** How do those closest to you perceive you, and how closely does their perception align with your self-image?

5. **Confronting Challenges:** Are there any difficult truths about yourself you've been avoiding? What are they? What is it about these truths that make them difficult to face?

6. **Rinse and Repeat Relationship Dynamics:** Are there recurring themes in your relationships that you've noticed? Identify them and try to make connections to the underlying causes or sources of these themes, such as your personality, attachment style, or past experiences.

Deep Desires And Life Goals

7. **Life's Desires:** What are you striving for in life? Share your deepest desires and what they mean to your sense of purpose.

8. **Aspirations and Dreams:** Which dreams do you hold close to your heart, and which ones seem just out of reach? Reflect on what ignites your passion.

Core Values And Beliefs

9. **Personal Principles:** What core values do you stand by no matter what? Discuss any instances where you've felt challenged to maintain these values.

10. **Circle of Influence:** Who are the people you love and care for deeply, and how do they reinforce what's truly important to you?

Personal Growth And Change

11. **Areas for Growth:** Where do you see opportunities for personal growth in your life? Where do you need to boss up? Identify these areas and why they matter to you.

12. **Lifestyle Adjustments:** What changes do you need to consider to better align with your desired life path? Reflect on the habits that shape your daily life.

13. **Past Influences:** How do your past experiences continue to influence your present? Explore their lasting impact on your life choices.

Acknowledging The Past

14. **Hurdles to Healing:** How can you proactively address and heal broken aspects of your past that continue to impact your present experiences and relationships? Imagine what wholeness might look like for you, then list some steps that will lead you in that direction.

15. **Facing Hard Truths:** What empowering truths can you embrace to embolden you to confront the more difficult ones? How can addressing them now benefit you?

16. **Fear Factor:** What fears are holding you back from living your life boldly? What steps can you take to confront these fears?

Spiritual Conversations

17. **Kickin' It with The King:** If you and Jesus were having a talk over coffee, what questions would you ask, and how do you think He might answer them?

Practice #3: Talk It Out

In the quest for self-awareness, an often-overlooked strategy is simply talking it out, and like any good practice, it starts at home. Yes, I'm telling you to talk to the most available person: you. Before you worry about folk questioning your sanity, I'm here to tell you that the right brand of self-talk is a mighty tool on your journey of self-discovery.

Think of it as conversing with your personal board of advisors: your very best friend, your most helpful critic, and your favorite motivational speaker all at once. Just maybe don't do it at full volume on the subway unless you want some side-eyes from fellow commuters. But on a serious note, self-talk is no joke. It's a power move for getting to know your innermost thoughts and feelings.

The key is to engage in constructive self-talk, where you show yourself grace, speak life, ask hard questions, and verbalize your goals and dreams freely. When you're faced with challenges or doubts, instead of resorting to self-deprecating comments like, "I can't do this," or "This is too hard," flip the script and say, "I've got this because God's got me," or "I can conquer anything with God by my side."

Amp yourself up when you're not giving yourself enough credit and bring yourself back into the present when you're brooding over the past. Check yourself when you're slacking. Tell yourself the truth when you need to get it together. Remind yourself of who you are in Christ when anxiety comes creeping in.

Don't stop at pep talks though. Go deeper. Hold a board meeting with your feelings, interrogate your motives like a savvy detective, and cross-examine your fears. Get to the truth of who you are—just remember to be both the good cop and the bad cop. Imagine God as a part of these conversations too. In Matthew 28:20, He promises that He's always with us, so you can trust that He hears you.

It Takes A Village: The Importance Of Outside Perspectives

And while your internal monologue might be so good it deserves a podcast, be sure to invite a peripheral panel of trusted advisors for some accountability. The truth is, we can be our worst critics, and at the same time our biggest enablers. That's why we need friends and mentors who can lend objectivity. We're wired for relationships, after all, and communication is the lifeline of connection. Believe it or not, we need to talk to others to stay sane. (Ever wonder why solitary confinement is a punishment?) Having external sounding boards keep us from losing our grip on reality. God Himself said it wasn't good for man to be alone. (Genesis 2:18)

Now, I'm not saying you should go around spilling your guts to everyone—that's not good either. The kind of conversations I'm telling you to have are not for gossiping or finding a sympathetic ear to co-sign your soliloquies of self-deception. They're not about monologuing your woes nor pontificating your opinions.

YOU MUST HAVE SELF-AWARENESS

I'm talking about reaching out to trusted advisors who balance hard truths with grace when you're off track and need redirection, or encouragement when you're on the right track but feeling fatigued. So, choose your council carefully, then actually listen to what they say. I mean really listen, not just wait for your turn to talk again. Check for disconnects between their perspectives and your own views about yourself, and if there is a disconnection, explore why those gaps exist.

Be open to their feedback even when it stings a little. You'd be surprised at how much you can learn about yourself through the eyes of someone else. A multitude of counselors yield wisdom (Proverbs 15:22), but only if you're willing to hear them out.

So, engage in these two-way conversations—within and with others—knowing they're both crucial to understanding the multifaceted being that you are. Admit you don't have all the answers alone; you need community. It's through this process that you'll refine your self-awareness, develop a closer relationship with God, and come through more alert to the path that is meant for you.

Practice #4: Observe And Be Mindful

In the pursuit of self-awareness, mindfulness is an essential tool. Mindfulness is having a heightened sensitivity to your present experience without judgment, attachment, or being overwhelmed by whatever feelings or emotions come up. To cultivate it, you've got to make a habit of observing yourself and your interactions with openness and curiosity. Tuning in to the current moment with impartiality is how you collect the evidence you need for self-awareness.

> **If experience is the best teacher, observation is its trusty assistant, and mindfulness is the diligent student taking copious notes.**

When you allow yourself to fully inhabit the present without the clutter of yesterday's regrets or tomorrow's anxieties, you become a credible witness, watcher, and observer of your own life.

In Luke 8:18 (CEV), Jesus says, "So pay attention to how you hear. To those who listen to my teaching, more understanding will be given. But for those who are not listening, even what they think they understand will be taken away from them." This reminds us that mindful observation unlocks wisdom and truth.

Actively listen and practice presence and you'll gain a deeper understanding of yourself. Ignore or half-listen, and you might miss out, or even lose what you thought you grasped. Be attentive with how you 'hear,' not just with your ears, but with all your senses, and most importantly, with your heart.

Catch Yourself In The Act: Mastering Mindfulness

You need to be present and engaged in your own life as you go about your day, paying attention to your thoughts, feelings, and bodily sensations. This will allow you to identify patterns, recognize biases, and make more conscious choices. Every experience—from the mundane to the monumental—is an opportunity to learn something about yourself.

By embracing mindfulness, you can:

- Sharpen your focus and improve your concentration.
- Deepen your emotional intelligence and empathy.
- Reduce stress and anxiety.
- Cultivate a sense of inner peace and well-being.
- Develop a profound sense of self-understanding.

As the saying goes, "The unexamined life is not worth living."

YOU MUST HAVE SELF-AWARENESS

At first, it might feel like hard work to be mindful. It is a practice that requires discipline and perseverance and it's easier to just give in to autopilot mode and let life pass you by in a whirlwind of routines and distractions. But if you want a better, more fulfilling life, you must engage with your life on a deeper level, and mindfulness is one of the skills you'll need. And what better way to engage with your life than to take a deep dive into your own self-awareness? It's time for a pop quiz.

Now that we've unpacked the importance of self-awareness and explored some strategies to cultivate it, come on and get real with yourself. This quiz is designed to shine a light on your self-awareness strengths and areas for growth. It's not about perfection; it's about honest reflection.

Before you dive in, set the stage. Find a quiet spot where you can tune into yourself without distractions. Grab a pen and paper, or open up a note on your phone. Take a deep breath, and commit to answering each question as authentically as possible. This quiz is for your eyes only, so there's no need to front. The more real you get, the more insight you'll gain.

As you read each question, take a moment to reflect before choosing your answer. Don't just go with your first impulse - really sit with it and consider how the question applies to your life. If you're struggling to choose between two options, go with the one that feels most true most of the time.

To calculate your score, tally up your points for each question, then, add up your total points and check out the scoring interpretations to get your self-awareness snapshot.

But don't just take your score and run. The real gold is in the "why" behind your answers. Take some time to journal about your reflections:

- What patterns do you notice in your strengths and growth areas?

- How have your self-awareness blind spots shown up in your relationships or decision-making?
- What's one insight from the quiz that really resonates, and how might you put it into action?

Remember, self-awareness is a continual journey of growth and discovery. Embrace the process and keep showing up to do the work. Your future self (and your future spouse!) will thank you.

Alright, enough pep talk. It's time to answer some questions.

How Self-Aware Are You?

1. How clearly do you understand your own core values, passions, and aspirations?

    a) Very clearly - I can easily articulate what matters most to me (4 pts)

    b) Somewhat clearly - I have a general sense but struggle to prioritize (3 pts)

    c) Not very clearly - my values feel a bit fuzzy and change frequently (2 pts)

    d) Not at all clearly - I feel out of touch with what I truly care about (1 pt)

2. When you experience a strong emotional reaction, how often do you step back and analyze what triggered it and why you reacted that way?

    a) Always - I consistently reflect on my reactions and their causes (4 pts)

    b) Sometimes - if it was a particularly intense or unusual reaction (3 pts)

YOU MUST HAVE SELF-AWARENESS

    c) Rarely - I get caught up in the emotion and don't usually analyze it (2 pts)

    d) Never - I just wait for the feelings to pass without examining them (1 pt)

3. How would colleagues or friends describe your self-perception compared to how they see you?

    a) Very aligned - others say my self-assessment is accurate and insightful (4 pts)

    b) Somewhat aligned - there are a few areas where others see me differently (3 pts)

    c) Not very aligned - others often point out gaps in my self-awareness (2 pts)

    d) Not at all aligned - I'm frequently surprised by how others experience me (1 pt)

4. How proactive are you about seeking out constructive feedback from multiple sources?

    a) Very proactive - I regularly ask for input and act on valid feedback (4 pts)

    b) Somewhat proactive - I'll ask for feedback when I face a big challenge (3 pts)

    c) Not very proactive - I mainly rely on unsolicited feedback if it comes up (2 pts)

    d) Not at all proactive - I tend to dismiss or avoid constructive criticism (1 pt)

5. How often do you engage in self-reflection practices like journaling, meditation, or discussing your challenges and growth with a mentor or coach?

    a) Very regularly - it's a core part of my personal growth routine (4 pts)

    b) Somewhat regularly - I make time for it when I can, but not always consistently (3 pts)

    c) Occasionally - I've tried it a few times but struggle to make it a habit (2 pts)

    d) Rarely or never - I don't prioritize dedicated self-reflection practices (1 pt)

6. Think of a recurring piece of constructive criticism you've received. How did you respond?

    a) I carefully considered it, sought more feedback, and worked to address it (4 pts)

    b) I acknowledged it but struggled to shift my mindset or behavior accordingly (3 pts)

    c) I got defensive and looked for reasons to discount or dismiss the feedback (2 pts)

    d) I beat myself up and wallowed in feeling inadequate without a growth plan (1 pt)

7. How attuned are you to the subtle ways that past experiences may be shaping your current assumptions, reactions, or blind spots?

    a) Very attuned - I often connect the dots between past and present (4 pts)

YOU MUST HAVE SELF-AWARENESS

    b) Somewhat attuned - I can see the influence if I step back and analyze (3 pts)

    c) Not very attuned - I don't naturally examine the roots of my reactions (2 pts)

    d) Not at all attuned - I focus on the present without tying it to the past (1 pt)

8. When you face a challenge or failure, how do you usually respond?

    a) I objectively analyze what I could do differently next time (4 pts)

    b) I acknowledge my part but focus more on external factors (3 pts)

    c) I get defensive and look for others or circumstances to blame (2 pts)

    d) I jump to self-criticism and pessimism about my abilities (1 pt)

9. How comfortable are you with acknowledging your areas for growth or mistakes?

    a) Very comfortable - I own them openly and work to improve (4 pts)

    b) Somewhat comfortable - I'll admit them if asked, but don't broadcast them (3 pts)

    c) Not very comfortable - I downplay or sugarcoat my weaknesses or errors (2 pts)

    d) Not at all comfortable - I get defensive and struggle to admit faults (1 pt)

10. How often do you step back and question whether your current habits and behaviors are aligned with your long-term goals and values?

- a) Very regularly - I frequently assess whether I'm walking my talk (4 pts)

- b) Somewhat regularly - I check in on this every few months or so (3 pts)

- c) Occasionally - I'll sometimes notice misalignments but not consistently (2 pts)

- d) Rarely or never - I don't really analyze my day-to-day against the big picture (1 pt)

Scoring And Interpretation:

- **35-40 points:** High Self-Awareness. You demonstrate strong self-awareness in both internal and external domains. You have a clear understanding of your values, regularly engage in effective self-reflection practices, proactively seek out feedback, and take ownership of your growth areas. Keep up the great work, and consider how you might mentor others on the self-awareness journey.

- **27-34 points:** Moderate Self-Awareness. You show good self-awareness in some areas, but have room for growth in others. Look for themes in the questions where you scored lower - do you need to strengthen your internal self-awareness through more robust introspection, or seek more external feedback to illuminate blind spots? Pick one area to focus on first, and set small goals to enhance your self-awareness in that domain.

- **18-26 points:** Emerging Self-Awareness. You're starting to build self-awareness, but it's not yet a consistent practice. You may rely more on unsolicited feedback than proactive self-examination, and struggle to translate insights into action. Start by adding one dedicated self-reflection practice into your weekly routine, whether that's journaling, meeting with a mentor, or taking a weekly self-assessment. Focus on staying curious about your blind spots and seeing feedback as a gift.

- **10-17 points:** Low Self-Awareness. Your self-awareness has significant room for growth in both internal and external domains. You may struggle to identify and articulate your core values, react to challenges from a place of defensiveness or self-criticism, and miss or dismiss valuable feedback. Commit to small, daily practices to build your self-awareness muscle, like setting an alarm to check in with your emotions, or asking one trusted colleague for one piece of constructive feedback each week. Seek out resources on growth mindset, self-compassion, and effective introspection techniques.

Was that intense, or what? Remember, no matter your score, the fact that you showed up to do this work means you're already well on your way to greater self-awareness. But don't let this be the end of your self-discovery journey. Take your quiz insights and put them into action. Whether that means carving out more time for self-reflection, seeking out honest feedback from loved ones, or working with a coach or therapist to unpack your patterns, every small step counts.

A Final Note On Self-Awareness

Think of your self-awareness as an app; it needs constant updates to function at its best. Keep your mind open and your curiosity alive. Stay interested and invested in the developments of your own story. Life never stops teaching, so you should never stop learning. It's like when the Apostle Paul tells us in Romans 12:2 (NIV), "Do not conform to the pattern of this world, but be transformed by the renewing of your mind."

As your inner world comes into view, imperfections will become conspicuous. Meet these shortcomings with self-compassion. Be patient, yet persistent. You should expect ebbs and flows in this journey of insight, as no season is the same. Some seasons will bring aha moments, others more subtle growth, but whether in stillness or suffering, your self-knowledge will deepen if you have eyes to see, ears to hear, a mind to understand, and a heart to receive.

When it feels like your progress has stalled or you keep facing the same battles, reexamine the lessons you previously learned to make sure you actually got the lesson. There's a reason we find ourselves in the same kind of situations (or with the same kind of partners) again and again.

Learn from past mistakes, then, let them go. Imperfection simply says you're human, and there's grace for that, but don't let that grace be an excuse to not improve the things you can. You have a responsibility to yourself (and whoever your future spouse might be) to show up for the hard work of growth and getting to know yourself better.

RULE 2
KNOW YOUR NON-NEGOTIABLES

Learn your non-negotiables, and you'll find that instead of losing yourself in the search for love, you'll be defining the very essence of the love you seek.

What Are Non-Negotiables?

Non-negotiables are the qualities, characteristics, and values that are essential for you in your future relationship. These aren't *nice-to-haves* but *need-to-haves*. You won't die without them, but you may experience a slow, relational death if you compromise them. They are the immoveable rocks in the stream of your dating life around which all else must flow for smooth sailing. They are the deal-breakers and deal-makers, the boundaries, and the standards that you set for yourself and a potential partner.

Non-negotiables serve as a roadmap that guides you through the dating world. Knowing and owning them prevents you from losing yourself while looking for love. They align you with partners who treasure what you treasure, which means that rather than miss out on spontaneous connections, you'll be better equipped to recognize when those connections truly fit into the life you want to build. These pillars help you filter out mismatches so you date with precision.

> **Your non-negotiables reflect not just who you are, but also who you're looking to become alongside someone else.**

If you've never dated or been in a serious relationship before, then identifying your non-negotiables might be a little more challenging. You may find that what you think is a deal-breaker is not such big of a deal after all. On the contrary, you may discover that what you previously considered insignificant is a major factor in your relational satisfaction. The dating phase is a time to test out your theories about what you think you need versus what you actually can't live without.

Ideally, the time to identify and establish your non-negotiables is before you start dating, so you can avoid making compromises later that might jeopardize what's most important to you. Also, having this foresight stops you from entering marriage under the mistaken belief that you can negotiate your way through fundamental differences, which are, in truth, dealbreakers.

That said, you should know that once you get married, whatever else marriage is, it's an ongoing negotiation—a lifelong series of compromises, and mutual adjustments. It's two people coming together, each with their own perspectives and needs, working to create a harmonious life together. Given this reality of constant negotiation in marriage, it's better to settle on the things you don't ever want to have to negotiate well before entering a serious relationship.

KNOW YOUR NON-NEGOTIABLES

The solitary work you do now may just lead to a shared triumph later, with someone who respects and appreciates your non-negotiables as much as you do.

To put it simply, non-negotiables determine your compatibility, commitment, and satisfaction in a relationship. They are:

- The criteria you use to evaluate and choose your potential partner.
- The standards you use to measure and maintain your relationship quality.
- The indicators you use to assess and improve your relationship happiness.
- The personal protectors that safeguard your present and future well-being.

Determining Your Non-Negotiables

When it comes to defining your personal non-negotiables, God's Word should be your first and foremost guide. As you seek Him first (Matthew 6:33), He will direct you to a joyful purpose and life, and that's whether you're single or married. If it is His will for you to wed, He's able to bring the right person along at just the right time who will both help you fulfill that purpose and add meaning to your life.

However, while your faith is where you start, it's not where you stop. You also have to think about how your age and gender might affect your dating options. God helps us see the big picture, but we live in a world where practical considerations matter too. As you move from reflecting on your non-negotiables at a spiritual level to exploring how they play out in your everyday reality, keep in mind that though your core values may remain constant, the way they manifest in your relationships may evolve over time.

Age-Related Realities

If you're a woman in the spring of your life, say 18-25, there's a good chance your non-negotiables read like a wish list as long as a CVS receipt and a checklist that came straight from your social media feed. You may require that a man be six feet with a six-figure salary and six pack abs for you to even look his way.

But with maturity comes pragmatism. My ladies who are a little older, you know that life has a way of refining your deal-breakers, softening the edges of your once rigid expectations. You recognize that some of the checkboxes of youth simply haven't held up over the years. The criteria you clung to fiercely in your twenties have lost their relevance and are not as essential as you thought. Qualities that once glittered with promise may now be dimmed by reality, replaced by attributes that speak to deeper, more substantial connections.

THE DATING DICHOTOMY: MEN VS. WOMEN

Black Women In The Dating Arena

Let's just talk straight. For black women looking to marry a black man, the dating scene can feel like a desert, parched and barren. Systemic issues like disproportionate incarceration rates, same-gender attraction, higher mortality rates, and men who are already in relationships make it tough to find a good man. This complex dating environment can make black women feel like they have no choice but to reassess their non-negotiables. I see you and hear you. The struggle is real and the frustrations are valid.

It's a mathematical reality that there are less men in the marriage market for you to choose from (unless you live in Alaska, North or South Dakota, Wyoming, or Colorado, where eligible men outnumber eligible women).[11] This means that it's quite possible that there are simply not enough men to go around. It stands to reason then that the most desirable men—those who are financially stable, emotionally mature, and spiritually grounded—may be in high demand but low supply.

Ladies, I know this seems so unfair, and keeping it all the way 100, it saddens me that this inequality exists in our communities. As a pastor and natural problem solver, I like to help people and I like solutions. I want to give people answers to their problems. Since I've been pastoring, however, I've encountered two significant challenges where conclusive answers elude me. The first one is not the topic of this work, but I'll mention it because it's part of the reason the marriage outlook for black women is what it is.

One, addressing the needs of same-gender attracted individuals who seek change—those who honestly see it as sin, and yet, like what they like; and two, helping the numerous wonderful women in my congregation find a partner who values them for who they are.

These two issues continue to weigh heavily on my heart. I don't have a foolproof formula for these challenges, no secret sauce to spoon-feed those who come to my church hungry for answers, and it drives me nuts. Other than telling them to stay abstinent until change comes, which feels quite inadequate at times, I don't have an answer.

What I do have though, is faith. Faith in our God's wisdom and faith in His promises. And while I might falter for answers, God has them all. He has a greater understanding of your needs, wants, and heart's desires than you could ever fathom. So even in the midst of uncertainty, I can tell you with confidence that if you are facing one of the two issues I described (or any issue for that matter), you can rest in the assurance of God's love and sovereignty. His timing, though often painstakingly slow by our watch, is always perfect. "If you have any kind of trouble in your mind, give it to God. God has promised to take care of you." (1 Peter 5:7 EASY)

Compromise vs. Critical Thought

Regardless of the odds, your attitude should never be, "I'll just take what I can get." Far from it! You deserve a man who is absolutely crazy about you and would go to the ends of the world to make sure you know it. God wants the best for you, and that includes in your romantic relationships. Don't lower your standards based on the fear that all the good men are being snatched up, but at the same time, be realistic about your options.

Here's where I want to make a distinction between compromise and critical thought. Compromise means settling for less than you deserve, while critical thought implies being more calculated and strategic with your decisions. Critical thought says, *here's the reality, here's my new reality, and here's how I'm going to adjust my non-negotiables to reflect this reality.* It's strategically adapting to circumstances while staying true to your principles.

In other words, let's say you really had a taste for a 12 ounce steak but because of a nationwide shortage, only 8 ounce steaks were available. Are you really compromising if you opt for the 8 ounce steak? Maybe it's not the exact steak you wanted, but if that exact steak isn't an option because it's not available, you choosing the best steak option that *is* available is not a compromise.

The truth is, you may have to adjust your non-negotiables to reflect demographic realities if you're serious about finding a partner. It may mean opening your heart to possibilities you may have ruled out previously. Instead of rigid checklists, think in terms of values, character, and spiritual connection. You may have to expand your options to include other cultures, consider a wider age range, and resist the urge to discount someone simply because they don't fit your preconceived image of an ideal partner.

Can I offer you language to help you reframe your mindset as you make this adjustment? This is not giving up—it's growing up. You're not settling, you're shifting based on an understanding of your reality. Don't mistake this as a green light to compromise on critical values or core principles. Rather, see it as an opportunity to redefine what is truly important to you in a relationship.

By identifying what matters most, you can expand your pool of potential partners who align with your values in meaningful ways. Hold firm on your non-negotiable core needs but remain open-minded around the peripheral. With thoughtful critique and honest conversations with your trusted advisors, you can discern which desires are flexible versus foundational to your fulfillment.

Black Men With Assets—You're In High Demand

On the flip side, for black men, the narrative differs. If you have Jesus and a job, you're a winning lottery ticket. There are countless beautiful women who want you right now, as there are more eligible women than men in most states. So, you are quite literally spoiled for choice. If you're great looking, that's a plus, but if you're not, it's probably not a deal breaker for the women you're interested in. The truth is, as long as you have the basics covered, you don't need to adjust anything you identify as a deal-breaker, so choose a woman who has all the features and qualities you like, in every single way. Don't settle for any woman who doesn't check all your boxes.

If it sounds like I'm telling the men, "Get everything you want," and telling women, "You might want to rethink what you want," I am. Let's be honest, ladies, if the shoe were on the other foot, meaning if there were millions of available men that met all your criteria, would you feel the need to adjust your list of needs and wants in a partner? It would almost be unintelligent to settle for anything less when you can have whatever you want.

Like it or not, this is the contemporary reality of dating, and even though some of these facts about male privilege and priorities may make you feel uneasy, I'm giving you major insight into the mind of a man. The question is, as a single woman who wants a man, knowing that the ratio of eligible men to women is skewed in favor of the guys, how do you use this information to your advantage?

I'll tell you what I would do. First, I would ask myself, are my standards core values or just preferences? Am I being too rigid and eliminating potentially excellent prospects? Am I more focused on the packaging than the content? Then, after making my list and checking it twice, I would do everything in my power to look the best that I can from head to toe and bet on myself.

The fact of the matter is you catch a man's eye by the way you look, initially anyway, not by how smart, funny, or anointed you are. So, invest in your appearance and put your best foot forward. Work on your health and fitness, elevate your style, keep your hair, nails, and skin well maintained, drink your water, mind your business, and present yourself with class.

I'm not telling you to change who you are. On the contrary, I'm telling you to fully embrace who you are. Maximize your external radiance to match the inner brilliance you already possess. A bit of extra polish doesn't hurt, especially when demand exceeds supply.

When you feel attractive, you emanate the confidence that comes from self-care. This energy is magnetic, drawing others to your light. Don't just hope for the best, take action to be your best self. The man who will cherish you is seeking a woman who cherishes herself. From physical fitness to fearless confidence, be relentlessly focused on continuous self-improvement. Don't stress trying to fit into a certain box or meet a particular standard. Instead, focus on expressing your femininity in your own unique way and walk like you know who you are.

But here's the catch: All this outward adornment does is get his attention. You have to be able to back it up with your character if you want to get him to even think about marrying you. As a woman, it's one thing to get a brother to bend *me*, it's another thing altogether to get him to bend *the knee*. He may be drawn initially by physical attraction, but what makes him stay and commit is who you are on the inside. So, while you're investing in your appearance, even more importantly, invest in your inner life.

The right man will fall in love with the full package—confidence, intellect, and spirit. These are the qualities that transcend outer beauty and set you up to secure lifelong devotion.

Sisters, love yourself fiercely so you don't seek validation from unworthy men. Become a whole woman with or without a man. Don't use your looks as a means to an end only, but as an expression of your self-respect. Shine your light for you. The rest will follow.

Time To Get Focused

Now, let's home in on the task of defining your non-negotiables, which requires introspection, prayer, and honesty. These parameters determine the trajectory of your relationships. Take a moment to carefully consider what you absolutely cannot compromise on. What are the things that you are not willing to negotiate under any circumstances? And I mean to the point that you are willing to be single for the rest of your life if you never found someone who met every single one.

I urge you to approach this list with realism and the chances of meeting someone who ticks every box. It's important to lean into your self-awareness when identifying your non-negotiables. Don't include superficial criteria that you know deep down aren't deal-breakers. For example, if you meet a great guy who's a millionaire but is 5'9" instead of 6'2", would that truly matter in the grand scheme of things?

CRAFTING YOUR NON-NEGOTIABLES: A COMPREHENSIVE APPROACH

Let's explore a few categories, including physical appeal, financial, personality, communication style, and more, to help you create a comprehensive list of non-negotiables. You can also refer to your self-awareness exercise for additional personal insights.

For The Fellas: Get What You Like Physically

Here's where I really want to go further with the men. In traditional heterosexual relationships, men tend to prioritize physical attractiveness more than women do. Now what one brother finds attractive may not be the same for another brother, but regardless of individual preferences, physical attraction is highly important for a man's long-term fulfillment and satisfaction in a relationship.

This may sound shallow, but it's not. It's honest. It's real. It's important. I'm writing this from my loins, my logic, and my leadership—this is nearly thirty years faithfully and joyfully married, plus well over the 10,000 hours of experience that "they say" makes you an expert. Physical attraction is a natural and necessary part of any romantic relationship. It's the spark that ignites the flame, the glue that binds the bond, the spice that adds the flavor. It's the thing that makes you feel alive, excited, happy, and satisfied. It's the thing that makes you say, "Mmph," every time they walk into a room.

Lust At First Sight

I'm going to be a bit graphic here and say that as a man, if the woman you're dating or considering dating doesn't make you want to smell, touch, kiss, lick, suck, and eat her, she's probably not your wife. It should feel like lust at first sight, so if you don't have to restrain yourself from going too far in your thoughts the moment you look at her, I'm telling you, you need to keep looking.

You're going to need this high level of attraction because of the reality and saturation of sexual imagery in our society, because you may want to reproduce, and because it's in our nature to desire the opposite sex. So, if you don't marry a woman who makes you feel this way, you may find yourself wanting something different when it's too late to get it. I didn't make *this* rule, I'm just delivering the message.

The rule I did make and suggest you follow is what I call the 90/10 rule. Make sure that the woman you're with looks better to you than 90% of the women you see. There's always that 10% who may look better, but as long as you're smitten by the one you're with, you won't be swayed by the rest.

I'm going to go out on a limb and say God wants you to lust after the woman you're going to marry. Lust is a healthy thing in the proper context. God is looking at your heart and your attitude. If you're out here just lusting after every woman you see, hooked on porn, or undressing women in your mind left and right, that's something altogether different and God is not okay with that. But the woman who you're evaluating to see if she has the potential to be your wife? God wants you to sexualize her.

This may be the realest, rawest thing you've ever heard a pastor say, but I did not write a third edition of this book to not be blatantly honest: I believe in some areas, we make God deeper than what He is. If you're on a mission to find your wife, and you see this woman who has everything you want physically, how can you not visualize her in that way? If you're a Christian brother, you have more pressure than a brother who's unsaved and doesn't care about marriage because he's going to get variety for the rest of his life. You only get one woman for the rest of yours, so this choice becomes critical. If a curvy figure is important to you, don't let no skinny mini convince you to compromise your standards.

I'm being a little playful here, but most fellas I know like a certain kind of figure and face, the kind that makes them do a double-take whenever they see it (single fellas, of course, not the married ones), which is why I tell single men, get what you like. Whether you like a slim woman with thick lips or a thick woman with slim lips; a woman who's tall and full-figured or one who is short and petite, a woman who has a different wig for every day of the week, or one who only rocks her natural hair, know your type, and don't feel guilty about not giving women who don't fit your ideal the time of day.

If there's a certain size that you like certain body parts to be, do not, I repeat, do not date a woman whose body parts are not that size. You're actually doing both of you a favor because it's unfair to her and unnecessary stress for you to have to try to force something that's not there. Whatever images you would google in your nastiest, weakest, most lust-filled moments, that's the type of woman you should pursue and date. If you're typing in your search engine "big booty Bertha," then don't even look at a woman with a small derriere. If you know you've got a thing for A cups, then keep it moving when you see a woman who is at least a triple D.

The last thing you want is to be in the position of having to ask God to perform a daily miracle to make you feel something that you don't because you chose not to get what you like. This always blows me away. Like, believe God for healing from sickness. Believe God to help her overcome her past trauma. But you don't have to believe God for physical attraction. You can handle that on your own if you do what I'm telling you to do before you get married.

KNOW YOUR NON-NEGOTIABLES

I'm dating myself here but some of you may remember *Jet* magazine. Men would wait all month for this magazine to hit the shelves because it was the most access we had to view a beautifully built woman, the *Jet* beauty. She'd be wearing a bathing suit or a little bit of nothing. Now, however, one could argue that the women we saw in *Jet* were modest compared to what we see on the Internet today, and rather than having to wait a whole month, all a man has to do is open an app on his phone and boom! Within seconds, there are 10,000 women with their assets exposed filling his screen. With so much temptation, I believe it's imperative, brothers, that you know your standards and maintain them. Find a woman who is finer to you than 90% of the women you see in media and in real life.

Ladies, here's the question you need to be asking every guy who steps to you, maybe not on the first date, but don't let yourself catch feelings before knowing the answer: "Do you lust me?"

Then, don't minimize it, don't over-spiritualize it, don't make it that deep. Ask him if you have everything he needs physically. Is it a struggle for him to keep his hands to himself because of how good you look to him? If he says yes, great! Feel free to proceed. If not, run. Don't bother trying to change him; he's just not that into you.

I know that may be hard to hear, especially if you're into him, but believe me when I tell you, you deserve to be desired. If a man does not look at you in the way I've described, he is not the one for you. You are a daughter of the King, made in His image—remember that. It's not about being the most glamorous or having the perfect figure, but about finding someone who appreciates you for who you are. Moving on from him as soon as possible is the best thing you can do for you and your future self.

Now, I'm not saying that physical attraction is everything to a man. It's not. It's not the only thing, it's not the lasting thing. It's not enough to sustain a relationship, it's not enough to overcome challenges, it's not enough to build a future.

But it's something. It's something that you should know is a non-negotiable, and something you should not ignore, overlook, or downplay. It's also something you should never negotiate, but that's Rule 3.

For The Ladies: Beyond Physicality

While women do value physical attraction, it often intertwines with other qualities that make a man alluring. Qualities such as confidence, a good sense of humor, and stability are potent attractors. And I don't mean financial stability alone—mental stability, emotional intelligence, faithfulness, and consistency are equally important. Now, that's not to say that a woman wants to be with someone who she finds physically unattractive, it just means that other qualities can make a man more attractive than he otherwise would be to her.

For example, if a man has that dog in him (and I hate to say "dog" because I'm an Alpha man but I know you'll understand the reference), if he walks with a self-assured stride that commands respect, if he smells good, makes you laugh, oh, and has a few dollars too, he doesn't have to look like Denzel, Idris, Michael B., or whomever it is women are swooning over these days, ladies will still go out with him and be completely content in a relationship, looks notwithstanding.

Case in point, Jay-Z didn't get with Beyonce for her money or her voice, and she didn't marry him for his looks or physique. Stop me when I'm lying. Bey could've been working at Walmart or McDonald's and he still would've tried to talk to her. And she might have thought Jay-Z was fly, but if he wasn't the G.O.A.T. of the rap game with the charisma and swag he has, would she have even given him a chance?

I'm not throwing shade at Jay either. Heck, I'm in the same situation. Trust me, I know my wife is not with me for my looks. But I strolled up on her, swag and confidence on lock, and when I took the opportunity to shoot my shot, I hit nothing but net. Next thing you knew, she was mine.

Whereas certain qualities in a man will make him more attractive to a woman, this is just not true for men. If we don't have that attraction for a woman right away, it doesn't matter how charming, sharp, or successful she is, she doesn't become more attractive to us. Men and women are just different in this way.

That said, ladies, get what you like physically as well, because you don't want to wind up with a man solely due to his wit or wallet and then find yourself cringing every time he tries to touch you. I've talked to many formerly married women who were in this kind of relationship and based on their sentiments, I can tell you that while singleness sometimes has its challenges, being in a sexless marriage is worse.

Physical attraction should indeed be a factor, it's just that the substance of the relationship is deeper than looks. Look for a man who brings out the best in you, whose presence makes you feel emotionally safe, whose conversation stimulates you intellectually, and whose reliability makes you feel secure.

Now, let's talk about some of the other areas where you'll have to determine what's negotiable and what's not.

BELIEFS AND ETHICS

Spiritual Harmony

For a successful and lasting relationship, you need to be on the same page spiritually. It's not just about what church you go to, it's about how your faith influences your daily decisions, your values, and directions in life. For instance, if you believe in waiting until marriage for sex but your partner doesn't... well, let's just say that could create a serious conflict. Divergent views here also reveal a deeper incongruity that could lead to strife and misunderstanding down the line. Remember, you're not just dating for the here and now, you're dating with the future in mind.

Character Counts

For both men and women, the character of a potential partner is a heavyweight in the balance of relationship non-negotiables. A person's character shapes how they treat you, themselves, and others around them. It influences how they handle stress, success, and setbacks.

Moral Compass

Agreement on principles and ethics is non-negotiable for many. This can include views on giving back, morality, political beliefs, and more. Misalignment can create a fundamental rift between partners.

Respect and Equality

Respect and equality are essential for a healthy relationship. A respectful partner will listen to your opinions, support your goals, and communicate honestly. An equal partner will share the responsibilities, decisions, and joys of the relationship. Without respect and equality, the relationship will suffer from imbalance, resentment, and conflict.

FINANCIAL FOUNDATIONS

Income and Spending

Reflect on your approach to money. What are your financial goals, and how do you prioritize spending and saving? A partner with a drastically different financial style could lead to conflict. Determine if financial discipline, a similar income level, or attitudes toward investment are non-negotiables for you.

Debt and Responsibility

Consider your stance on debt. Is being debt-free or having a plan to manage debt a non-negotiable? Assess how much financial baggage you're willing to take on, as it can affect future decisions like homeownership, travel, and even retirement.

Lifestyle and Ambitions

Your desired lifestyle is also a key factor. Do you long for luxury, comfort, or simplicity? Can you be with someone whose aspirations are significantly higher or lower than yours?

PERSONALITY TRAITS

Temperament and Behavior

Think about the personality traits you resonate with. Do you need someone who's optimistic, ambitious, upbeat, or calm? Traits like these deeply affect daily interactions and long-term satisfaction.

Conflict Resolution

How a person handles conflict can be a deal-breaker. Do they approach disagreements with a willingness to resolve them constructively, or do they resort to anger or avoidance? Find someone who approaches disagreements with the intent to resolve them, not win them. This trait can be the difference between a resilient relationship and a fragile one. A compatible conflict resolution style is often a non-negotiable.

Growth and Flexibility

Is a growth mindset important to you? Consider whether you need a partner who is open to change and personal development. Stubbornness or a lack of willingness to adapt can be a sticking point in relationships.

COMMUNICATION STYLE

Openness and Honesty

Effective communication is the lifeblood of any relationship. Decide if you need someone who communicates openly, with honesty and clarity. Without this, misunderstandings can fester and grow.

Listening and Understanding

It's not just about how someone talks, but also how they listen. A partner who truly hears you and strives to understand your perspective can be a non-negotiable aspect of a healthy relationship.

Expression of Affection

Determine how important verbal affirmations and discussions of feelings are to you. If you need a partner who is verbally expressive about their love and affection, this should be on your list. Also, consider your need for intimacy and emotional connection. Is it important to you that your partner openly show their emotions, or are you more comfortable with a less demonstrative approach?

Frequency of Physical Intimacy

Reflect on your natural inclinations and instincts. What do you consider ideal when it comes to physical intimacy, and what are your preferences when it comes to physical touch? Is a couple times a week enough for you or do you prefer daily expressions of physical affection? You want to be clear here, as conflicting ideas or desires in these areas can lead to tension, hurt feelings, and emotional distance over time.

LIFESTYLE AND HABITS

Health and Wellness

Your health habits, including diet, exercise, and substance use, are significant. Compatibility in this area can impact daily living and long-term health.

Social Life

Are you social or a homebody? Your non-negotiables should include the social rhythm that suits you best. A mismatch here can lead to dissatisfaction on both sides.

Hobbies and Interests

While you don't need to share all hobbies, having some overlap or at least an appreciation for each other's passions can be a non-negotiable for a fulfilling partnership.

FUTURE PLANNING

Children and Family

Views on family planning are often non-negotiable. Whether you want children, the parenting style you aspire to, and how you envision your family dynamic are pivotal points. In addition, if you have children from a previous relationship, it's not unreasonable to expect your potential partner to not just tolerate, but accept and love your children. If he or she isn't willing to fully embrace your kids as their own, it's a wrap. If you don't have children, (or even if you do) and don't want to raise someone else's, dating a single parent is off the table.

Career and Relocation

Your career goals and openness to relocation can be make-or-break factors. If you're firmly rooted in your career or location, a partner must be on board with that reality.

Prioritize And Highlight Your Non-Negotiables

Once you've hammered out the broad strokes, break it down even further. Literally make a numbered list. Top 5, Top 10, Top 25, whatever you need to feel confident that anyone who makes the cut has the makings of an amazing mate. Which items are crucial? Which can you be flexible on? Weigh their significance, ponder the trade-offs, and consider how these elements will affect your partner possibilities.

In Summary

The categories outlined in the previous section include some examples of non-negotiables that you may have or encounter in your dating and marriage journey. Of course, there are other non-negotiables that you may have or discover, and you'll need to modify this list based on your own unique needs and preferences. Creating this list is not about setting constraints as much as it is about paving a path to true compatibility and contentment.

The key is to be super specific about what you require in a mate. Don't be vague. Get granular. For example, don't just say you want someone faithful. Define what faithfulness looks like to you—no flirty direct messages on social media, no suspicious "close friends" of the opposite sex, etc.

Make sure to dig beneath surface-level traits too. Don't just say you want a God-fearing man. How does his faith show up in his day-to-day life? Is Jesus just a t-shirt he wears once a week, or the crux of his character? You get the idea.

KNOW YOUR NON-NEGOTIABLES

While every married couple will have to work to understand each other better, being in sync in central areas ahead of time lays a secure foundation. By considering these facets of life and relationships, you can determine what you need in a partner versus what you're willing to navigate together. Identify which is which, then communicate and stick to them no matter what.

This is what we're going to cover in **Rule 3 | Never Negotiate Your Non-Negotiables.** Because trust me, there will be times when you meet someone so fine, so charming, and so cool that you'll be tempted to bend your own rules and blur your boundaries. But when you do that, you're not just negotiating what's important to you, you're also negotiating your worth. How so? Keep reading and learn why surrendering your non-negotiables is a cost too high, even for love.

RULE 3
NEVER NEGOTIATE YOUR NON-NEGOTIABLES

"Compromise for your dream, but never compromise on your dream." -*Imran Khan*

Don't let infatuation cause you to minimize issues that could become major points of contention later. Know what's acceptable and what's absolutely not for your future happiness.

We established in Rule 1 that self-awareness is key to determining your non-negotiables, and in Rule 2 that your non-negotiables act as your personal relationship guidelines. Your non-negotiables are not just a checklist of preferences, but a reflection of your deepest values and needs. Let's quickly recap.

THE IMPORTANCE OF NON-NEGOTIABLES

- **Self-Understanding:** Knowing your non-negotiables requires a deep understanding of yourself. This self-awareness is critical as it ensures you don't lose yourself in a relationship by settling for things that don't align with your core values.

- **Boundaries:** Non-negotiables set clear boundaries. They help you communicate to potential partners what you will and will not tolerate, preventing misunderstandings and setting the tone for mutual respect.

- **Compatibility:** Non-negotiables are key indicators of compatibility. When both partners have a clear understanding of each other's non-negotiables, they can better assess the potential for a long-term, satisfying relationship.

- **Avoiding Resentment:** By sticking to your non-negotiables, you avoid future resentment. Compromise in these areas can lead to dissatisfaction and regrets, potentially undermining the relationship over time.

Self-Awareness And Authenticity: Knowing Yourself To Uphold Your Standards

While it's possible to love someone without a high level of self-awareness, clearly, I don't recommend it because you can't accurately identify your non-negotiables without it, and if you can't identify them, there's no way you can sustain them. That said, being aware of your non-negotiables is one thing, honoring them is another.

It's true that many people, if not most, enter relationships with low self-awareness because they don't know any better. But if you ask those who've been there, done that, sold the merch, and wrote the memoir, they will tell you how hard of a life that can be.

Loving without self-awareness often leads to heartache. Loving with self-awareness and still choosing someone who negates your non-negotiables is a different kind of heartache.

Self-Awareness Without Serious Adjustments Is Self-Sabotage

Without the commitment to make serious adjustments once you've identified your non-negotiables, all your self-reflection will have been in vain and this kind of self-awareness is, in essence, self-sabotage. Let's talk about why and how to make sure you're clear on how to move from awareness to action, realization to resolution.

Self-awareness is to singles what a map is to a traveler. It shows you where you are, where you want to be, and even how to get there, but what it doesn't do is move you forward.

As a single person, your self-awareness is peppered with milestones and landmarks that point to your desired destination, but if you ignore them, you'll stay stuck where you are. Or you'll waste time and energy on detours and dead ends and just be lost, confused, and frustrated. Knowing your non-negotiables is useless if you don't uphold them when you're dating. Being aware of unhealthy patterns is fruitless if you repeat them.

The Signs Of Self-Sabotage

Even when you know yourself, you may find yourself falling for someone who, deep down, you recognize is wrong for you. You tell yourself it doesn't matter that they have dealbreakers X, Y, and Z. You downplay red flags and suppress doubts, shushing your own discontent with the false comfort of companionship and rationalizing that you can negotiate your non-negotiables or change them. It's a toxic loop of rationalizing and settling.

Despite knowing your standards, you fail to walk when lines get crossed. Why? Fear of loneliness makes you cling to unworthy partners. Anxiety about finding someone new paralyzes you from moving on. Low self-worth convinces you that you can't do better.

So, you start making excuses.

"Maybe I'm being too picky."

"He drinks a lot but not as much as my ex."

"She's bad with money but hey, nobody's perfect."

Bit by bit, you loosen your boundaries to accommodate their flaws. If you find yourself trying to cover for your partner's behavior or mistreatment, explaining away disrespect, criticism, or neglect, that's self-sabotage.

This is a painful path. Pursuing mismatched love may temporarily fill the void of loneliness, but you sentence the relationship to dysfunction by denying truths you already possess about your needs. This is conscious self-betrayal. It severs you from your essence and erodes self-trust. Clarity without change is self-sabotage.

The Repercussions Of Stagnant Awareness

Another thing to consider is that when you don't act on your self-awareness, you're not just standing still—you're stepping back. Each time you compromise a non-negotiable for someone, you send a message to yourself that your needs aren't valid or attainable; that they or their needs are more important to you than you and yours. By putting their desires ahead of your own well-being, you're communicating that you don't believe you deserve to have your standards respected. You're saying, "My worth is flexible."

But the devil is a lie because it most certainly is not! You deserve respect and you are worthy of having your boundaries honored. Staying when your boundaries are routinely crossed causes toxicity in relationships. It robs you of inner peace and emotional safety. You teach others how to treat you by what you're willing to accept. If you wait around hoping a person will change, you'll only dig yourself deeper and likely experience more of the same. What motivation does a person have to change if they're not experiencing any consequences for their actions? And threatening to walk away but never following through is worse, as this will only cheapen your words and strengthen a person's conviction that they can continue crossing your boundaries without repercussions.

Break Free Into Fulfillment

Enforcing your standards, on the other hand, is an act of self-love. You're asserting, "I know what I need to feel safe, valued, and fulfilled in a relationship, and I will not betray myself by not honoring these needs."

Making serious adjustments based on your self-awareness requires courage, discipline, and resilience. When someone violates or doesn't fit with your non-negotiables, you must be willing to leave. You have to trust that maintaining your boundaries will lead to greater happiness in the long term, even if it hurts in the short term.

This adjustment phase can feel lonely, but you can take comfort in knowing that you are making a commitment to yourself, a declaration that you won't sabotage your chances of finding the relationship you really want by settling for the one that's most convenient right now. You're foregoing self-sabotage in favor of self-fulfillment, ensuring that the self-awareness you've worked so hard to cultivate results in the love and respect you inherently deserve.

When You Compromise, Your Credibility Crumbles

You should also consider that every unjustifiable concession you make diminishes—if not damages—your self-esteem and sends the message that your non-negotiables are in fact quite negotiable after all. You're conditioning yourself to accept things you would normally reject, which will translate into other areas of your life as well.

In dating, if you start compromising your non-negotiables, one day you're going to wake up waist-deep in wackness, wondering how you got there. Even compromising on small things sets the stage for bigger concessions down the road. You let a man get away with flaking on a date, next thing you know he's flaking on your anniversary and calling it "no big deal." If you allow a woman to constantly belittle your aspirations, soon enough you'll find yourself doubting your ability to achieve anything at all. Before you know it, you're stuck in a cycle of unfulfilling relationships disconnected from your core values.

Red flags are tests, not suggestions. Pay attention early and often. Your non-negotiables are your guardrails, protecting you from crashing or veering off course. Value yourself enough to uphold them.

The Ripple Effect Of Compromising Core Values

Furthermore, if you have children or plan to have some with your spouse in the future, compromising core values won't just affect you, it will affect them too. If Daddy thinks going to church is stupid, guess who's going to Sunday soccer instead? A father who rejects church shapes his kids' spirituality. A mother who downplays the importance of abstinence teaches her sons and daughters to do the same. Marriage reveals; it doesn't reinvent. What you tolerate won't change post-wedding.

The Importance Of Integrity In Your Non-Negotiables

This is also why you want to be careful with what you put on this list, because once you say something is non-negotiable, you owe it to yourself and the other person to stick by your word. Don't say anything that you already know you might compromise on.

For example, don't say that smoking is a deal-breaker, and then date somebody who always has a cigarette in one hand and an asthma inhaler in the other. That's hypocritical and should send you running for the hills, not leaning in for a goodnight kiss. If you told Jerome you don't date smokers, then his weed breath shouldn't suddenly become a breath of fresh air. He's out here exposing you to second-hand smoke, and you're acting like it's Kool.

And we all know a Marcie who said her man had to be a faithful churchgoer, then ended up with Deon who only sets foot in church for weddings and funerals. That's despite her praying and fasting for a God-fearing man. *Marcie, girl, that's not a faithful churchgoer; that's a seasonal visitor. You let Deon with his suave looks and smooth talk sweep you off your feet and now your standards have slipped like a kid on a water slide at summer camp. Sis, who's gonna take you seriously in the future? Not Deon. You're not even gonna take you seriously.*

And I'm not picking on the ladies, fellas do this too. They compromise on the things they really want in a mate, things that should be non-negotiable, for reasons we're going to get to in a moment.

Physical Attraction Revisited: A Biblical Perspective

I've spent a great deal of time emphasizing how important physical attraction is to men and why. After walking with married and single men alike for over two decades, there's one thing I'm 100% sure of: For the majority of men, physical attraction is the first attraction.

To those of you who read my first work, you might even remember that Rule 1 used to be, "There Must Be Physical Attraction." I haven't moved on that; I've just broadened it. I know it may sound superficial or unspiritual to some, let me suggest to you that it's biblical. Beauty and attraction for men throughout the scripture are very important factors.

Abraham's wife, Sarah, was so beautiful that Abraham feared the Egyptians would kill him just to have her (Genesis 12:10-20). This was a woman so beautiful it made a grown man fearful for his life. Then Genesis 24:16 refers to Rebekah, Isaac's wife, as "very beautiful."

Isaac's son, Jacob, is so captivated by Rachel's beauty when they first meet that he labors seven years just to win her hand in marriage. Genesis 29:17 says, "Rachel was shapely and beautiful," and Jacob was so smitten with her beauty, he felt those seven years "seemed like a few days" because of his love for her. (Genesis 29:20)

Even Bathsheeba, who King David spotted bathing, is described as "very beautiful" in 2 Samuel 11:2. Then there's Esther, who won her king's heart with her beauty and became queen. (Esther 2:17)

Need more proof? Consider the Songs of Solomon, where two lovers continually affirm each other's good looks and strong desire for one another, in lush, vivid detail. This book of the Bible is practically a love song dedicated to physical attraction and the power of romantic love.

How beautiful you are, my love! How your eyes shine with love behind your veil... Your lips are like a scarlet ribbon; how lovely they are when you speak. How beautiful are your feet in sandals... Your breasts are like gazelles, twin deer feeding among lilies... The curve of your thighs is like the work of an artist. (Song of Solomon 4:1,3, 5; 7:1, GNT)

This man wasn't just talking about her inner beauty; he was clearly captivated by her outer beauty as well.

Likewise, she goes in on how handsome her man is to her: "My lover is handsome and strong; he is one in ten thousand. His face is bronzed and smooth; his hair is wavy, black as a raven." (Song of Solomon 5:10-11, GNT)

And ladies, how about King David's son Absalom? He was described as the most handsome man in Israel. 2 Samuel 14:25-26 (ESV) says, "Now in all Israel there was no one so much to be praised for his handsome appearance as Absalom. From the sole of his foot to the crown of his head there was no blemish in him." Now, that's some description, is it not? Absalom probably could've been the cover model for *GQ - Ancient Jerusalem Edition.*

The Bible doesn't just tell us about these things for spicy bedtime stories. These are truths embedded within the scriptures about the value of intense physical passion, appeal, and beauty.

Gerald's Story: Gambling On Physical Attraction Is A Losing Bet

I mentioned previously that I know pastors who are in unfulfilling marriages because they ignored (or were oblivious to) the importance of physical compatibility. Well, one brother I counseled, let's call him Gerald, is a prime example on why you never want to compromise in this area. His reason for compromising? He assumed physical attraction would develop over time. His result? Let me just tell you his story.

Gerald always said he wanted a woman who was thick with a Coca-Cola bottle shape. A sister with confidence and a touch of sass, you know, the holy and hood type. But then he got with a woman, let's call her Teresa, who's sweet and smart as can be, but built like a spoon and meek as a mouse. I don't mean this as a slight to Teresa. She's beautiful inside and out, she just doesn't at all fit the body or personality type that Gerald claimed he wanted.

At first, Gerald figured physical attraction would grow over time. He thought because Teresa had so many other amazing qualities—level-headed, generous, loyal, easy to talk to, and filled with the Holy Ghost—that the fact that she didn't have the physical features he was into wouldn't matter as much. He thought that because they were such good friends, their emotional and mental connection would eventually ignite sexual attraction too.

Only it didn't, and six months into marriage, Gerald came to me frustrated, lamenting that he couldn't get excited in the bedroom. I looked at him with a raised eyebrow and said, "Bruh, you think? You married someone who you're not physically drawn to, and you wonder why you can't perform?"

Gerald's predicament is one I've seen time and again in my experience as a pastor and relationship counselor. Behind closed doors, countless married men have confided in me that they are with a wonderful woman who they love, like, and respect, but for whom they feel nothing for when it comes to sex. Gerald, and other men like him, don't seem to understand how foundational physical chemistry is in a marriage, especially for a man.

I felt for him, as I do for the other husbands, and even more for their wives, who presumably married them under the belief that they had everything they needed to keep their husband sexually satisfied. Why would they have had reason to believe otherwise? Why would a man marry a woman to whom he is not physically attracted?

Sadly, men do this all the time and when I ask them why, without fail, I receive some variation of one or more of the following answers:

1. **They believe it will materialize eventually.** This was the case with Gerald. Based on my research and experience, anecdotal and academic, it appears that physical attraction

is anthropological, meaning it's innate and for a man, as I explained in Rule 2, it's instantaneous. He either instinctively desires a woman or he doesn't, and the desire for what he inherently finds attractive doesn't disappear or change when or because he gets married.

Imagine trying to force yourself to love the taste of a vegetable you've never really liked. Let's say broccoli. Sure, you might learn to tolerate it, even enjoy it occasionally with the right seasoning, but that delicious, mouth-watering excitement you feel for a juicy steak? Broccoli will never give you that feeling and you're still going to find yourself yearning for that steak. Men hoping to grow in attraction after marriage end up disappointed when the chemistry never materializes. Initial lukewarm interest stays that way.

2. **They believe other qualities will overcompensate.** Like Gerald, some men think that because they have compatibility with a woman in one area, say, spiritual or intellectual, it will overshadow the lack of physical attraction. They might think that because she's goal-oriented, thoughtful, or a great cook, these positives will compensate for missing chemistry. But this thinking is erroneous because…

Relationships aren't algebra: You can't simply substitute variables and think everything will work out the same.

3. **They settle for the first woman who shows serious interest.** After having a string of unsuccessful attempts at securing a relationship, some men eventually settle on the first woman to reciprocate their effort or interest, even though she doesn't have the physical attributes they had previously professed were non-negotiable. They compromise on physical chemistry just to have someone checking for them.

4. **They feel like they've hit the jackpot. Literally**. Now, I must be honest and say no man has ever been bold enough to come right out and admit this to me, but I've seen it happen enough times to recognize it. Some men will marry a woman who's not their type physically because she brings financial stability they don't have. She may come from a wealthy family, have a lucrative career, or give him social status because of how well connected she is. Financial security or lifestyle become more important than physical chemistry.

   But this too, is a mistake because just as we cannot force our taste buds to enjoy broccoli over steak, we cannot fool our bodies into feeling attracted to someone who doesn't turn us on. A man who marries a woman for her money or status knowing that he's not attracted to her or gets with her because he's looking for a quick come-up is a bum anyway, and I say that with all the Christian love in my heart.

   Ultimately, he's going to be miserable, having weaseled his way into an all-expense-paid, five-star vacation... to a place he never wanted to go. The resort might be plush and the food amazing, but he's still stuck in a place he doesn't want to be.

5. **They feel pressure from their church.** In some contexts, the church, bless its heart, can push men to marry hastily. Pastors often cite Paul who says in 1 Corinthians 7:9 that it's better to marry than to burn with passion. The intention to preserve purity before God is good, but the pressure can lead to bad decisions. I'm reminded of the quote, "Never make permanent decisions based on temporary feelings."

   Desperate to avoid "falling into sin," some men marry when there is no physical attraction even when they know it's important because they believe that if the woman is also a believer, they can make it work. Maybe through the power of the Holy Spirit. However, without physical attraction, the relationship is doomed to fail. A man who marries a woman he is not attracted to will never be able to fully enjoy her company, and he'll always be wondering what it would be like to be with someone he is truly attracted to.

6. **They just don't know how crucial it is.** This one makes me scratch my head a bit, but it's surprisingly common. Some men simply don't realize how important physical attraction is. Even though we live in a hypersexualized culture, even though many men struggle with pornography and lust, some guys genuinely don't realize what a big deal physical attraction is in a marriage until it's too late.

   They assume attraction will happen automatically when the time comes for intimacy, that it can be negotiated, or that it matters less than shared faith, values, and life goals. So, they prioritize the practical on paper and figure passion will follow. When a man realizes how misguided he was in these beliefs, he might try to make himself desire his wife through sheer hope and willpower. He learns the hard way, however, that you can't reason, guilt, or force your way into sexual feelings for someone you are not physically compatible with.

The Consequences Of Compromising On Physical Attraction

Vows don't transform platonic affection into consuming desire and these kinds of marriages lead to restlessness, resentment, and rejection over time. Lack of mutual desire will permeate everything eventually. And unlike women who can feign desire and fool a man into thinking she enjoys sex with him when she really doesn't (not saying that she should, just saying that she *can*), because a man's sexual organ is on the outside, faking it isn't even an option. You can't pretend to have an erection.

The point I'm trying to make is there is no amount of commitment or effort that will change what you want in someone physically, so know what you like and love yourself enough to get it.

The Role Of Non-Negotiables In Safeguarding Your Sanity And Sacred Calling

Another reason why never negotiating your non-negotiables is so pivotal in the pursuit of romantic love is that we each have a spiritual assignment that transcends our earthly relationships. It can't be sidelined, ignored, or suppressed without leaving a deep hole in our souls that no amount of romantic love can fill.

In Jeremiah 1:5 (NIV), God says, "Before I formed you in the womb, I knew you..." and in Psalm 139:13-14 (NIV), David says, "For you created my inmost being, you knit me together in my mother's womb." From these scriptures, we can deduce that God has, in His infinite wisdom and design, ingrained in us a unique calling. This blueprint is a mark of our individuality, hardwired into us and carrying our distinct purpose. Our non-negotiables act as a guardrail for both our sanity and our sacred calling.

Here, the impact of compromising our non-negotiables is so profound that when they are ignored or compromised, we experience deep distress, desolation, and even depression because we're now disconnected from not only our authentic self, but also our life mission.

Remember, your non-negotiables reflect your core values, needs, and desires—all key aspects of who God designed you to be. Compromising them means compromising essential parts of your identity. Therefore, living a life that pushes these aside means living a life that's not fully yours.

The daily strain of managing a misaligned relationship will sap your spiritual strength and distract you from the things that could bring you contentment. Suppressed regrets and simmering issues steal focus, time, and mental energy that could be poured into meaningful work. Rather than unlock your full potential, you imprison it behind a facade of conformity.

When you compromise your non-negotiables then, you do more than just adjust your personal preferences; you potentially alter the course of your divine trajectory. Trying to force an inharmonious bond will throw your whole life off-key. Inner discord affects your ability to discern and follow God's voice. You lose touch with your intuitive compass.

Settle For Less And You Will Achieve Less

God's assignments require faith, courage, wisdom, and selflessness to fulfill. But spiritual depletion breeds faithlessness, apathy, confusion, and self-preoccupation. When core values go unsatisfied, you cannot be your best self. Your calling becomes an afterthought, not your driving force. Settling for less than what you need jeopardizes all you're meant to achieve.

In this light, to compromise on your non-negotiables is to gamble with the very nature of your divine purpose. It's to say that fulfilling someone else's desires is more important than fulfilling the plan God has for you. Do you seriously want to tinker around with your God-given DNA in the hopes of fitting into someone else's mold?

Honor Your Individuality—And Theirs

You were not created to blend into the backdrop of someone else's narrative or merely play a supporting role in their life. You're meant to be the protagonist in your own story, co-authoring with God a life that is not just good, but extraordinary. Ephesians 2:10 (NLT) reminds us, "...we are God's masterpiece. He has created us anew in Christ Jesus, so we can do the good things he planned for us long ago." A masterpiece is not to be adjusted to fit another frame—it is to be treasured, protected, and presented in its full glory.

In these last three chapters, we've talked a lot about the importance of knowing ourselves, our worth, and our non-negotiables. But for a relationship to start off on the right foot and continue to thrive, it's equally important to understand that the person you hook up with also has their own sense of worthiness based on their individuality and God-given assignment. Partnership is as much about two people coming together to fulfill each other's needs and desires, as it is recognizing and acknowledging each other's unique capacities and limitations.

The Parable Of The Pitcher And The Cup

This brings me to a demonstration I often do to illustrate this idea of recognizing and respecting each other's capabilities and competence.

With a pitcher of water in one hand, I sit an empty cup on a table in front of me. I start pouring water from the pitcher into the cup, narrating the process. "In the beginning, it's all good," I say, as the water begins to fill the cup. "The pitcher is happy to give, and the cup is happy to receive."

But then, of course, the cup reaches its limit and the water overflows. "Uh-oh. Now we have a mess. You're frustrated because you're a whole pitcher trying to pour into a cup. But how can you be mad at a cup for being a cup? It's not the cup's fault that it doesn't have room for your pitcher-sized expectations." I go on. "Did you not notice when you were dating that he wasn't that smart? Did you not see that she was shallow, or were you too busy focusing on her behind?"

By this point in the illustration, the audience is nodding, laughing, recognizing the picture I'm painting. "I hear it all the time," I continue, recounting a complaint some singles I've met have expressed.

Mimicking a puzzled expression I say, "But Pastor, I'm not that quick."

"You don't need to be. Just find someone that matches your speed."

I lift the pitcher and cup for everyone to see. "This," I say, pointing, "is about understanding and accepting each other's capacity. You can't force a pitcher's worth into a cup and then be upset when it can't hold it all. It's about finding someone who matches your pace and personality, and building a relationship that complements, not compromises, your individual identities. When you do this, you don't have to worry about negotiating that which shouldn't be negotiated."

Your non-negotiables determine if a relationship gets clearance for takeoff or denied at the gate. If you say something is non-negotiable, no matter how cute they are, how much money they have, or how much they appear to want you, if they don't meet that standard, you keep it moving. Stick to your list and don't let just anyone slide into your heart.

Upholding Your Non-Negotiables

As we've discussed, identifying your non-negotiables is the first step, maintaining them is what matters. Here's how you do it:

- **Communicate.** Openly discuss your non-negotiables early in the relationship. It's important that your partner understands what matters most to you and why.

- **Be Consistent.** Remain steadfast with your standards. If you've identified something as non-negotiable, treat it as such consistently, or risk blurring the lines on what is truly important.

- **Introspect.** Regularly reflect on your non-negotiables. As you evolve, so might your perspectives. Ensure they still resonate with your current self and life direction.

- **Choose Wisely.** Select partners who respect and share your non-negotiables. This shared respect creates a strong foundation for a relationship that can weather life's challenges.

In Summary

Self-awareness gives you the clarity to define your non-negotiables. Once defined, non-negotiables help you separate the wheat from the chaff, the seeds from the weeds. They are the commandments of your relationship journey. Sticking to them takes conviction, courage, and sometimes sacrifice, but it saves you from far greater pain down the road and brings you closer to the love you want and need.

One final note about why you should never negotiate your non-negotiables: Compromise starts on the first date and never stops. Next thing you know, you're twenty years in, staring at a man or woman you don't recognize—I'm talking about you, not your partner. I want better for you. Don't settle for less than God's best just because you're impatient or insecure. You deserve the real thing.

And now let's get into **Rule 4 | Don't Play Date - Date on Assignment.**

RULE 4
DON'T PLAY DATE - DATE ON ASSIGNMENT

> "...Of the three options of singleness, dating, and marriage, dating is by far the least fun. By far. If you are having a blast dating around, you're probably doing it wrong."
>
> - Jonathan Pokluda, *Outdated*

Play Dates Are For Kids

As someone who's walked alongside countless Christian singles, if there's one thing I've learned, it's that the way we approach romance as Christians must be fundamentally different than the world around us. While society embraces a carefree hookup culture, we are called to a higher standard that honors God. Far too often, however, too many of us treat dating like we're flipping through channels, looking for a show that might catch our interest for a night of binging or perhaps a season of indulgence in our guilty pleasure.

I'm not here to sugarcoat it. I'm here to tell you that as Christians, this isn't the move. We're not in the business of play dates; we're in the kingdom business of seeking a lifetime partner. To 'date on assignment' means that every interaction, every conversation, and every moment you spend with someone you're considering as a potential life partner is intentional. You're not in this just to see where things go. You've got a direction, a purpose, and, above all, a clear end goal in mind.

Dating on assignment isn't nearly as enjoyable as dating for entertainment or temporary pleasure. If you're having too much fun, you're probably not doing it right because truth be told, Christians don't date to have fun, fill weekends, or distract from loneliness. We date for one reason and one reason only: to find a person to marry.

Purpose Over Pleasure: The Seriousness Of Christian Dating

If this sounds intense, that's because it is. Dating is a serious step towards marriage, and marriage is a sacred vow before God. In this chapter, I'm going to show you how to date with the seriousness and spiritual focus it deserves. Trust me, when you start dating on assignment, you'll see how it changes the game entirely – for the better.

Your dating life shouldn't feel like a revolving door of potential partners. You want a specific someone who will amplify your mission, multiply your joy, and divide your burdens. Based on the work we did in the first three chapters, you know that this can't be just anybody, so you shouldn't date just anybody.

Your search for a soulmate should be sacred, selective, and strategic.

Adopting this sentiment should filter out any frivolous contenders who are not ready to level up. To date on assignment is to be savvy and shrewd. It may sound more like I'm giving you tactical business advice than dating advice but that's because we are talking about investing your most precious resources after all—your time, your energy, and your heart. The objective is to minimize your risk of emotional pain and pointless encounters while optimizing for the most productive and God-honoring dating experience you can have.

Play dating, also known as casual or recreational dating, is dating with no clear purpose (other than having fun) or commitment and the pitfalls of this approach stretch far and wide. It may seem harmless at first — a coffee date here, a movie night there. But before long, this pattern can lead to a tangled web of emotional attachments that lead you into some messy situations that leave you confused and heartbroken. Without intentionality as your anchor, you'll drift into questionable entanglements that cloud your judgment and compromise your values.

Blurred Lines And Broken Hearts: Casual Dating Casualties

Get too comfortable with that cutie and next thing you know those physical boundaries get real blurry, real fast. When there's no defined commitment or set direction, the temptation to be intimate can escalate rapidly. To that end, you should never hangout with someone of the opposite sex who you're attracted to without a game plan and some sort of accountability measures in place. This could mean having a trusted mentor or friend who knows the ins and outs of your dating agenda, someone who keeps you on track and helps you guard your heart.

THE TEN RULES OF DATING

When wandering hearts meet wandering minds with no kingdom vision in view, that's when danger creeps in.

You might even consider setting reminders on your phone to check in with yourself about your intentions and actions. All this might sound like a lot of work, but that's because it is work, remember? You're on assignment.

You might think you're strong enough to be all alone with bae and not get caught up, but do not give yourself that much credit. You will end up in bed and increasing your body count. Many a good Christian have fallen into sexual sin simply because they put themselves in tempting situations without an exit strategy. Don't be one of them. Protect your body, mind, and spirit.

Further, hanging out over time promotes sharing, bonding, and emotional disclosure. Play dating can yoke real feelings to false attachments and lead to painful breakups down the road. We are not toying around with people's emotions or letting them toy with ours. You see, when dating becomes a sport, the heart becomes the playing field, and the consequences can be more significant than we realize.

When you're out here in these dating streets, you've got to remember that you're dealing with God's handiwork. People aren't just random products for you to pick up, use, and discard at your leisure. No, these are living testimonies to the Creator's genius, each one bearing His image and deserving of your utmost respect. When you fail to acknowledge this, when you treat them like they're just a means to an end, you're not just disrespecting them - you're disrespecting the One who made them. We've got to do better than that. We've got to recognize the sacredness and seriousness of what we're engaging in.

If you know in your spirit that you're not feeling a person enough to move forward with a serious commitment, don't lead them on through continuous contact. Don't be the guy or girl having fun at someone else's expense or using them for selfish personal gain.

The Dater's Downward Spiral: From Casual To Uncontrollable

Even if you manage to dodge the physical and emotional snares, casual dating can easily become an addictive habit that distracts you from finding your true person. And let's not forget about the precious time and energy you'll be wasting. Play dating can consume your life, as you go on endless dates leading to nowhere. It's a never-ending cycle of disappointment and frustration. Your time and energy are valuable. Don't waste them on connections that won't bring you any closer to a meaningful relationship.

> **Idle time and undefined relationships are the devil's playground. Don't get caught slipping.**

Play dating can also hinder your healing process. If you've been hurt in the past, jumping from one casual fling to another will only prevent you from fully healing. Instead of addressing your emotional wounds and resolving any lingering issues, you just cover them up with distractions. Those wounds will resurface sooner or later, however, if you don't give them the care and attention they deserve.

At the end of the day, play dating is unfair to both you and your date. It shows a lack of self-control and disrespect for the heart of another. As Christians, we're called to honor God with our bodies and in our relationships, not just in our words, but through our actions. Your relationships are a reflection of your faith, and every date should honor that faith. When you date on assignment, you're not just scouting for companionship; you're seeking a partner who will stand beside you in God's service, someone who will join you in the trenches of life's battles as well as in the triumphs. This is a far cry from the trivial pursuit dating is often reduced to.

One At A Time Please: Dating As A Single Elimination Tournament

For a moment, let's entertain the practice of dating in the context of sports. In basketball, a single elimination tournament is where you're matched against one opponent at a time. Each encounter in this tournament, much like each date in real life, is a distinct round and you know how it goes: one game, one chance to advance, which means that each game demands everything you've got. It's like the playoffs. That's how I want you to date—like you're in the playoffs of your life and each person you meet could be your teammate in the finals, in marriage.

You wouldn't play two basketball games at once, right? Of course not. So when you're dating, at no time should you be seeing more than one person at a time. You're not lining up multiple opponents to see who might eventually challenge you; you're giving your full attention to the one right in front of you.

Why? Because every individual you choose to spend time with deserves your thoughtful consideration. When you're with someone, be all in. This person might just be the one you've been praying for, the one God has chosen for you, which means you could be on the start of a journey that leads straight to the altar.

Reel In The Right One

Fellas, let's cut to the chase—literally. I know the pleasure of pursuing multiple women can feel like a rush but believe me when I tell you that nothing beats the joy of catching the right one. This is what you're after: the ultimate catch. You don't get the ultimate catch by casting your net wide, in any old kind of water, and reeling in everything you can. No, you get the ultimate catch through targeted fishing, dropping your line in the most promising waters at just the right time.

I know the world tells you to "play the field," "test the waters," and offers you a crock of other contemporary clichés that encourage you to be indecisive, non-committal, and even manipulative. But let's be real. Would you want the woman you love—the one who will mother your children—to be treated this way by another man? No? Then don't treat any woman that way.

Be selective about who you spend your time with, only dating women who share your spiritual values and relationship goals. If you're on a date, that means she's already passed the physical attraction test. Great. You're now looking for substance and shared vision for life. Stay alert for signs that indicate poor character or immaturity. Guard your heart until you're sure you've found a true partner worthy of your commitment.

Weed Out The Time-Wasters

Ladies, I know it feels good to be pursued and have your options open. But real talk -quantity over quality is a bad dating strategy. Don't mistake surface level attention for meaningful intention. Spreading yourself thin emotionally may provide temporary validation, but it won't reveal God's best pick for you. Rather than casually entertaining a stream of suitors, be more selective and really take the time to know them. Vet thoroughly for the qualities most vital in a husband and father if you have kids or want to in the future. Don't be easily wooed by charming words and flashy gifts. Let a man prove himself over time through his actions and consistency.

Ladies and gents, keep your eyes on the prize – which is a relationship that honors God. When you step onto that court, or onto that dating scene, your focus should be laser-sharp, your strategy well thought out, and your purpose crystal clear. Approach each interaction without the distraction of backup options on the sidelines competing for your interest. And when you find that person who's just as serious about this as you are, who's running the same race towards God, you'll feel it. That's when the game really gets good, so get out there and date with purpose. Play to win – God's way.

The Assignment Mindset In Practice

To date on assignment is to recognize that every date isn't just an encounter but a crossroads—a chance to determine whether the path ahead is one you should walk together. It means engaging your heart, but also your head and your spirit, asking the tough questions and seeking discernment at every turn. You approach each potential relationship with the sober-mindedness and conviction that this could lead to a covenant before God.

While dating on assignment isn't necessarily supposed to be fun, it doesn't have to be a joyless journey. Think of it as a more sophisticated form of dating, elevating the process to something more substantive than mere amusement. It invites the Holy Spirit into your decision-making, opening the door for God-honored attraction and genuine love, which outlasts the temporary stimulation of its more inferior counterpart - infatuation.

Your First Date? It's Recon Time, Soldier

When dating on assignment, the excitement is in finding your divine mate, your partner for life. Every conversation, every outing is more than just getting to know someone. Instead, you're evaluating whether they fit into the life God has planned for you.

That said, your first date is a fact-finding mission, your very own recon operation to gather intel and collect as much information as possible to help you determine whether this person might be the one. Keep in mind that it's an interview though, not an interrogation, so keep the conversation light and engaging, allowing it to unfold naturally and flow both ways. This is your opportunity to learn about your prospective partner's values, dreams, and character. You're there to connect, to share, and to listen.

If you're a parent, you're on double duty. You're not only evaluating them as a companion for you but as a bonus parent, role model, and guide for your children as well. This adds layers to your assignment, making it crucial to take your time and lean heavily on discernment. Listen to how they talk about family, their openness to your children, and their general attitude towards parenting roles. These cues can be subtle, but they're incredibly telling.

Assess their potential influence and integration into your family. Their interaction with your kids, even in hypothetical discussions, holds invaluable insights into their parenting style and understanding of family dynamics. Can you see them playing catch in the backyard with your son or helping your daughter with her homework? Do they have any habits that you wouldn't want your children to pick up? The answers to these questions could be the deciding factors on whether to move forward or end the date.

Treat Your First Date Like A Job Interview (Because It Kind Of Is)

It's important to remember that while you are doing your investigative work, they are likely doing the same with you, trying to consider how you might fit into their existing or desired life structure. In this dance of mutual discovery, it's best to embrace this opportunity to be as transparent as possible.

Talk about your life, your ambitions. Be open and honest about who you are and what you value. If you're passionate about your career, own it. If you're a homebody who values quiet nights in, say that. Don't play down important parts of yourself to try to score points with them. Pretending might win you the moment, but it won't secure the future. Authenticity allows you both to assess compatibility accurately.

Remember, however, while honesty is necessary, oversharing on a first date could be just as detrimental as hiding the truth. There's no need to divulge every last detail of your life history or explain every bad decision you've ever made. It's sufficient to share enough to give a fair representation of who you are and what matters most to you. As time goes on and trust develops, deeper layers of vulnerability can be explored.

As they share about their life, assess whether their values align with yours. Do their goals inspire or resonate with you? Do they light up when discussing family or do they barely mention it? Are they respectful, thoughtful, and considerate in their words and actions?

Also, observe their body language and energy as you chat. Do they seem engaged or distracted? Do they carry a sense of peace or restlessness about them? Are they asking relevant questions or just waiting for their turn to talk?

In my experience, dating on assignment can feel like walking a tightrope—you're constantly balancing your desire for love with wisdom and discernment. It's the combination of hopeful expectation and cautious evaluation. You're excited about the possibility of them being a solid prospect, but you also understand that you need to curb your enthusiasm, so you can figure out if they are a solid prospect.

Still, first dates are a time for the collection of data, not a declaration of devotion. Take a long view and release any pressure to determine whether this person is your future spouse in one night. Just keep an eye out for any glaring no-gos. If none show up, then continue the conversation on subsequent dates as you both deserve the chance to reveal the breadth of your personalities over time. If something feels off, however, trust your instincts and call it. No harm, no foul.

Ending A Date With Grace

The only reason you should go on a second date is if you were totally impressed on the first one. Not every date will lead to a lifelong commitment, and that's okay. Obviously, it's not supposed to. But when it's clear that the relationship isn't part of God's plan for you, end it with integrity. Speak plainly but compassionately. Let them know that while you enjoyed meeting them, you do not feel the connection you're looking for.

For men, here is one way to end a new date kindly: "I want to thank you for allowing me to take you on a date tonight. I've enjoyed getting to know you, but I don't sense we were meant to be more than friends. I believe you're a great person, but I also believe we're looking for different things. It was nice to meet you/hang out with you and I wish you all the best."

This approach acknowledges the good while also being clear and honest about your feelings. Use whatever words you want, just speak sincerely without blame or criticism. A woman hearing this may feel like rejected, but she'll be eternally grateful that you didn't use her.

Women, you can also communicate your feelings gracefully without causing unnecessary pain: "Thanks for a pleasant evening. I truly enjoyed our conversation and the opportunity to get to know you. I think you're a wonderful person with a lot to offer, but my gut tells me we're not quite the right fit. I'm gonna get going now, but I wish you well."

This lets him down easy while still being direct about not wanting to continue seeing him. Speak from the heart but stick to the facts: you don't feel a romantic connection, your relationship goals aren't the same. Leading with gratitude and ending with well wishes shows consideration.

While uncomfortable, honesty provides closure to both individuals. It's not callous rejection, but rather gentle redirection towards God's best for each of you. However you choose to end things, do it maturely and quickly. If there are other plans for the night, cancel them. When ending a date because a person isn't a believer, be especially gracious. Your kindness may plant seeds that blossom down the road. Separation often stings, but in time, you'll realize necessary endings[12] often lead to better beginnings.

Playing For Keeps:
The Strategy Behind Dating On Assignment

In this chapter, we've discussed the concept of dating on assignment, a purposeful approach to seeking a lifelong partner that aligns with God's plan for your life. This isn't the world's way of dating; it's intentional, strategic, and rooted in faith. Dating on assignment transforms the entire experience of searching for a mate into a spiritual discipline that can lead you to your God-sent sweetheart. Take it seriously and keep your eyes on the prize – finding that person who will stand by your side, not just for a season, but for a lifetime.

Now that you've got these dating strategies locked down, you're ready to move confidently into the next chapter, **Rule 5 | Have The Jesus Talk**. It's time to lay down the foundation of faith that will underpin your future relationship. Get ready for a deep dive into discussions of devotion that will set the stage for a love that's as strong as it is sacred.

Allow me to leave you with one final gem before we close the chapter. Here's a 6-point game plan to seal the deal on mastering the art of dating on assignment.

Bonus: A 6-Point Game Plan For Dating On Assignment

1. **Set Clear Intentions:** Begin with the end in mind. Acknowledge that the ultimate goal of dating is to find a life partner who complements your faith and life mission. This is not about casual encounters; it's about working towards a future together.

2. **Ditch the "All You Can Date" Buffet:** Define what "dating on assignment" means to you and how you will implement this in practical terms. Savor meaningful connections rather than indulging in a spread of fleeting flings.

3. **Communicate Openly:** Be upfront about your intentions with those you date and seek the same level of openness from them.

4. **Stay Alert for Warning Signs:** Be vigilant in noticing behaviors that may indicate a lack of alignment with your values or life goals.

5. **Practice Patience:** Understand that finding the right partner may take time, and be willing to wait for God's perfect timing and match for you.

6. **Exit with Elegance:** If it's not meant to be, end things with kindness and honesty. It's not just about being respectful; it's about being Christlike, ensuring both parties can move forward positively.

RULE 5
HAVE THE JESUS TALK

"How can two people walk together unless they agree?" – Amos 3:3 (GNT)

The Love Affair That Matters Most

So far, we've discussed the importance of self-awareness, knowing our non-negotiables, never negotiating our non-negotiables, and dating on assignment. None of these strategies will be fully effective or lead to God's best unless we secure them with a solid spiritual foundation.

That brings us to **Rule 5 | Have the Jesus Talk**, and this is where I want to underscore the significance of shared faith in Jesus Christ. Explore what authentic spiritual connection looks like and how to assess if you truly share spiritual values with a potential partner.

But before I get into more dating advice, I want to first address a truth that threads the entirety of this book: a flourishing life, and ultimately, a flourishing relationship, begins with a personal relationship with Jesus Christ.

I'm taking it for granted that since you've gotten this far, you are a believer. You've accepted Jesus as your Lord and Savior, you're living out your faith, and you're aware that every stage of the spiritual path offers fresh revelations. What I'm about to share next is more for non-believers; however, stick with me. The assertions ahead will likely resonate richly. It will reaffirm truths you know, water seeds already planted, and maybe even sow some new ones for future growth.

This Is Your Come To Jesus Moment, Literally

If you haven't yet taken the leap of faith, let me, as a pastor who cares deeply about your eternal journey, extend an invitation to you. It's my heartfelt desire that you discover the greatest love there is—the love of Jesus Christ.

You're reading this because you want to know how to date and marry well, right? Well, let me make something abundantly clear. The journey toward a sacred union with another is as much about your vertical love affair with the Creator as it is about any potential horizontal love with a partner. I'm not suggesting that you seek an intimate relationship with God in *lieu* of a romantic relationship, but rather in advance and in anticipation of it. Here are four reasons why the sequence matters.

First, the love that Jesus offers is unlike any other love. It is peerless in its perfection. This Love left heavenly realms to walk among humanity. Though Jesus was without sin, He willingly took on ours, surrendering His body to be nailed to a tree to secure our forgiveness, defeat death, and redeem our lives. This Love brought us into existence, understands us completely, and desires us unconditionally. This Love is so powerful that despite knowing the worst and messiest parts of our us, Jesus looked beyond our brokenness and blemishes and said, "You are worth dying for."

It is this agapē love that teaches us what godly love looks and feels like. Our partners, as wonderful as they may be, can't meet all our needs, let alone fill the deepest longings of our soul. But this love, and only this love, can. It can satisfy your innermost desires, heal your deepest wounds, and fulfill your wildest dreams. Once you comprehend the promise of this love and the boundless grace and goodness that comes with it, your understanding of what it is to experience real love will never be the same.

Second, when you build and base your life on a loving relationship with God, you have access to a reservoir of joy and peace that can never be depleted by external circumstances. Even the best earthly relationships, including marriages, can bring moments of disappointment, pain, and heartbreak. When things get thick, you'll be glad you have the unfailing love of Jesus to cover you and fill in the gaps and fractures caused by human frailty and fallibility.

Third, you learn what it means to extend and receive God's brand of grace-filled, life-giving love. You have a heightened sensitivity to superficial substitutes and will be less likely to make the mistake of falling for someone who isn't ready or capable of loving you in the way you should be loved.

Fourth and finally, a fulfilling relationship with Jesus takes pressure off your future spouse. You realize that your most powerful source of contentment dwells within you—in your relationship with Jesus—so you don't go looking for it in their arms of another person. You don't expect someone to "complete" you because you're already complete in Christ.

When you feel lonely, lost, or untethered, you may crave the reassurance of a companion's comfort, but you won't confuse it for a cure.

You know that ultimately only closeness with our Creator can provide the solace and security you seek.

It is for all these reasons that I hope you would give Jesus a chance and allow Him to win your heart; that you would walk hand-in-hand with the Lover of your soul from this moment forward. His perfect love brings freedom, reassurance, and the confidence to be at ease in whatever state you're in (Philippians 4:11), whether you're single or married, thriving or struggling, in great health or enduring some challenges. The joy of knowing Him personally and walking with Him daily is unparalleled.

So, if you haven't already, won't you invite Him in your heart today? With a sincere prayer, you can receive His incredible love right now. It can be as simple as:

God, I need you. I admit that I am a sinner, and I need your forgiveness. I believe that you sent your Son, Jesus, to die for me, and to rise again for me.

> I want to accept Him as my Lord and Savior, and to follow Him with all my heart. I want to experience your love, your peace, and your purpose for my life.
>
> Please come into my heart and make me a new creation. Thank you for loving me, and for saving me. In Jesus' name, amen.

By offering this prayer, you've started a journey that will ready your heart for God's transformative work within you and through you in all your interactions. As you embrace Jesus or rekindle that connection, you're in a beautiful position to understand how your personal faith will light up every part of your life, including your future relationships.

Now lock in right here, because this is where I transition from my invitation to salvation to my goal for this chapter: that you would make knowing Jesus a prerequisite for anyone you date. It's essential that you have a personal relationship with Jesus, but it's just as crucial that your potential life partner does too because while faith starts individually, it blossoms relationally. This means you need to look beyond outward displays of religiosity to assess true spiritual compatibility.

A person who goes to church faithfully may seem like a diligent disciple of Christ. But this is not always the case. Just as savvy readers don't judge a book by its cover, true believers don't equate church attendance with character.

Simply clocking in at church doesn't signify spiritual depth, membership isn't a measure of discipleship, and regular attendance doesn't mean consistent growth.

You can frequent a place without being changed by it. You can go to the gym every day but if you're just there to snap selfies, you won't see any changes to your body. Similarly, if you go to the library every day but never crack open a book, you're not going to soak up knowledge by osmosis.

Church is no different. Weekly visits without genuine surrender to God, without seeking His wisdom, or striving to live according to His teachings is just spiritual window shopping. There will be no growth, no transformation. You might know church so well you can plan the order of service, predict when the pastor is going to pause for emphasis, and recite the lyrics to every praise and worship song, yet remain as distant from God as ever.

You see, the difference between a spectator and a participant at church is the same as the difference between a tourist and a resident in a city. Both are in the same place physically, but only one is truly engaged, invested, and making a home in that space. A tourist visits for a short time, takes in the sights, and then leaves. They may enjoy the experience, but they don't have a stake in the city's future. They don't contribute to its growth or share in its challenges. They're just passing through.

A resident, on the other hand, is connected to the city. They live there, work there, and build relationships there. They care about the city's future because it's their future too. They're not just visiting; they're part of the community.

So, when you're dating, you're not looking for the spiritual tourist. You're seeking the resident — the person who has made a home in their faith, who is rooted in and committed to God. To do this, you need to look beyond a person's Sunday habits to determine the authenticity of their faith and if your values and spiritual walks truly align. It's their Monday through Saturday lifestyle that will give you a clearer picture of who they truly are.

Understanding True Spiritual Compatibility

Spiritual compatibility, in the context of a Christian relationship, is that soul-deep connection where Christ isn't just a part of your lives; He's the commander of your joint mission. It's when your individual faith walks not only harmoniously coexist, but also strengthen and sharpen each other. This bond goes beyond religious practice or participation—it wraps around these key elements:

- **Christ at the Core**: You've both got Jesus as your foundation and it's more than just belief. He's your Alpha and Omega, the reason you get up and push through. He's the driving force behind every decision, the ambit of your moral code, and the guiding light in every storm.

- **A Vision for Victory**: Y'all are not just dreamers, you're dynamic doers with a vision. You've got spiritual ambitions that sync up seamlessly—like two arrows shot in the same direction, aiming for that Kingdom target. This may include growing in your faith, serving in ministry, or raising a family in a Christ-centered home. Your spiritual goals guide your life goals.

- **You Walk It Like You Talk It**: Living out your faith is a daily commitment. It's prayer in the morning, Christlike conduct by day, and reflection at night. When you're spiritually compatible, you and your partner hold each other accountable to this commitment of walking the straight and narrow path.

- **You've Got Each Other's Back**: A spiritually solid couple uplifts and encourages each other. You hold each other up and hold each other down, but never hold each other back. When one of you stumbles, the other says "I got you" and you restore each other with truth and grace. They celebrate spiritual wins together and continually refine each other. They're equally yoked pushing each other towards Christ.

- **You Worship and Serve Together**: Whether it's hands-up in worship or hands-on helping out, you serve as a team. More than just something you do, it's part of who you are. You find joy and purpose in being God's hands and feet together, whether at home, in your church, in your community, or beyond. It doesn't mean you're always together or that you're even doing these things at the same time. It does mean that you're harmoniously engaged in the work of faith, each enhancing the other's spiritual walk.

- **Prayer, Your Power Move**: A spiritually compatible couple believes in the power of prayer. It's having that partner who's riding with you and getting down on their knees to wage spiritual warfare with you or on your behalf.

You pray for and with each other, about everything. Prayer is how you fight your battles and how you win them.

These are just some of the markers of a couple that is spiritually compatible and prepared to embrace both the blessings and burdens as one. They're in it together for the highs, the lows, and the grow-throughs.

Faith At The Forefront Of Love And Life

As Christians, faith touches all aspects of our lives. Our beliefs shape our perspectives, priorities, and daily practices. Who we are flows from whom we serve, and this foundation informs how we choose to show up every day. In other words, our faith can't be compartmentalized—it's integrated into the way we live and love.

> **For the believer, at some point or another, spiritual compatibility will emerge as the most important factor in your relationship.**

When you wed your life to someone else's, your individual values and beliefs will inevitably merge or clash with theirs. Choose someone who is on the same page in earthly and spiritual matters, as your present and future well-being depends on it. The enemy, always lurking in the shadows and waiting to strike, will target you and your marriage. Make no mistake: He is hell-bent on tearing you apart, his intent to deceive, divide, then devour you.

When you lose a loved one, get let go from your job without warning, or get hit with a serious medical diagnosis, I can guarantee you won't be focused on your partner's good looks, sense of humor, or money. You'll be far more interested in whether they can intercede for you, remind you of God's promises when doubt starts to creep in, and help you weather the vicissitudes of life without losing your mind. It's during these trying times that the true value of spiritual compatibility is felt.

If your marriage is fortified by mutual faith and scriptural truth, the enemy won't stand a chance. When he comes for you, he will have to flee, finding himself outmatched and outwitted against the impenetrable force of your united spirit.

The spiritual principles you live by naturally impact your shared life, including the way you communicate, resolve conflicts, make decisions, handle finances, raise children, express intimacy, cope with challenges, celebrate wins, and navigate life overall. Your happiness, holiness, joy, and character become intricately linked with your partner's.

The Jesus Talk

With the basics of spiritual compatibility covered and the understanding that having a shared, sold-out faith with your partner is clutch, we're now ready to break down the point, parameters, and purpose of having what I like to call, *The Jesus Talk*.

The Jesus Talk is an honest, comprehensive exploration of faith, inviting you and your partner to pose and respond to questions that delve into the substance and authenticity of your spiritual journeys. It's a heart-to-heart exchange about your beliefs and convictions that should not be taken lightly because it is the litmus test for whether you both truly share the same spiritual foundation.

This is a conversation that will likely unfold over several interactions, so pace yourself. There's no need to try to cover everything in one sitting. But do make it a point to start these discussions early on. More on that later.

While casually chatting about God's goodness with friends might come easily, having focused, faith-centered conversations to gauge spiritual compatibility can feel daunting. It might feel a bit uncomfortable at first, as faith is often seen as a private matter, akin to politics - not typically a topic you broach over dinner when you're just getting to know someone. But when it comes to assessing a potential life partner, knowing where they stand on both faith and politics is non-negotiable.

It's understandable to feel nervous about having such a personal discussion, especially since the person might even end up revealing some views that don't mesh with yours. Push past that unease because it's better to feel discomfort now than regret later.

Difficult conversations pave the way for discerning decisions. Share your spiritual beliefs and listen closely as they share theirs. If your views are in sync, feel free to keep nurturing the connection. If not, consider redirecting your romantic energy elsewhere.

Trust in God's guidance throughout this process. If it's meant to be, a little awkwardness now will give way to spiritual closeness as you build trust and understanding.

Practicalities Of Having The Jesus Talk

Now that you understand the importance of The Jesus Talk, you might be wondering, "How do I actually have this conversation with my potential partner? What should I say? How do I approach it?" Don't worry. I've got you covered with some practical tips on how to initiate and navigate this crucial discussion.

- **Timing is key:** Don't wait until you're in too deep emotionally to have The Jesus Talk. The sooner you have it, the better. Ideally, this conversation should happen before you start officially dating, when you're still in the getting-to-know-each-other phase. Remember, delaying this conversation won't change the outcome and having it early will save you both time and energy.

- **Prepare well**: Pray and ask God for wisdom, guidance, and courage. Think about what questions you want to ask your potential partner, and what answers you expect or will accept.

- **Set the tone**: Choose a place that's quiet enough for a meaningful conversation, public enough to keep it comfortable. A coffee shop, a park bench, a quiet table at the back of a restaurant – these are all good stages for The Jesus Talk.

- **Ease into it:** Turn the conversation to spiritual matters naturally. Listen for an organic place to transition the conversation, maybe when you're talking about other values, and say something like, "Faith is really important to me. How about you?" Ask open-ended questions that require thoughtful answers, such as:

    o   How did you come to know Jesus?
    o   What makes you feel close to God?
    o   What are your spiritual goals?
    o   Where do you struggle spiritually?
    o   What kinds of situations test your faith the most?
    o   How do you feel about going to church? About serving in ministry?
    o   How do you feel about *insert any spiritual topic that is important to you*?

- **Be respectful**: Your aim here is not to judge anyone's faith journey; you're trying to discern whether it lines up with yours. Be careful not to come off critical or condescending with your questions. Don't interrupt or dominate the conversation, and if things start to get heated, pull back. You're not trying to get pulled into a debate where you have to defend your beliefs or where they have to defend theirs, nor are you trying to corner them into conversion or confession. If it gets to that point, then you already know everything you need to know.

These pointers are here to guide you into a forthright and fruitful discussion about faith. As you adapt these suggestions to your unique communication style, keep in mind that this dialogue is meant to be ongoing and it should progress and deepen as your connection does, *if* your connection does.

Approach the conversation with a spirit of reciprocity and openness. Be prepared to not only ask probing questions but to answer them with equal candor. While there's no need for a tell-all memoir, be transparent about your struggles, mistakes, or areas for improvement. The goal is to be as truthful as possible, which means you also shouldn't exaggerate or sugarcoat your faith, act as someone you are not, or pretend to believe something you don't. Own where you are and give your partner the opportunity to be attracted to your spiritual authenticity.

Prove It: Using The Fruit To Gauge The Root

If a person claims to be a believer when you meet them, don't let their proclamation be enough. Make them prove something. A good barometer for a person's spirituality is a solid juxtaposition of what they say to what they show. Bible readers know that Galatians 5:22-23 lists what we call the Fruit of the Spirit. (I tell our church all the time that you can also call it the Proof of the Spirit.)

> **Galatians 5:22-23 (NLT) 22 But the Holy Spirit produces this kind of fruit in our lives: love, joy, peace, patience, kindness, goodness, faithfulness, 23 gentleness, and self-control. There is no law against these things.**

If you don't see these characteristics in a person, there is a good chance they don't have a genuine relationship with Jesus and are not spirit-filled. I would really consider moving on quickly and not settling for less than God wants you to have.

Pitfalls Of Surface-Level Faith

Now, you might be thinking, "Pastor, this sounds good, but what if it's a person who I go to church with already and who I've had the chance to observe in ministry? Isn't that enough? Do I really need to get this deep?"

No, it's not enough and yes, you do need to get this deep. Without a deeper investigation, you can't simply assume you're on the same page spiritually. People can make big claims with their words, and from afar, it can seem like they even back them up with their actions. You need to have some up-close conversations to verify you share common ground in this area. There is a big difference between outward signs of faith and authentic spiritual commitment and if you mistake the former for the latter, you are setting yourself up for trouble.

Here are some of the outward signs of faith that people often display:

- Going to church regularly or occasionally
- Reading the Bible occasionally or rarely

- Saying they believe in God, "The Big Guy Upstairs," or a "higher power"
- Praying before meals or in times of need
- Wearing a cross or a religious symbol
- Posting inspirational quotes or scriptures on social media
- Volunteering for a cause
- Being nice, polite, or friendly to others
- Using familiar church catchphrases

In most cases, the behaviors on this list are good signs, but because they can easily be copied without any real conviction or commitment, they're not enough to prove that someone has a true, personal relationship with God, nor enough to determine if someone is spiritually compatible with you.

In fact, these outward signs can be done for all the wrong reasons, such as:

- To impress you or others
- To fit in or belong
- To avoid conflict or criticism
- To gain favor or advantage
- To ease guilt or conscience
- To escape reality or responsibility
- To follow tradition or culture
- To please parents or family

Outward religiosity without inward transformation is deceptive. Some folks wear their faith like it's a fashionable accessory—it looks good on the outside but that's about it. Beware of confusing church activity for spiritual depth and being fooled by this facade of faith. It's flimsy. It doesn't hold up when tested.

Surface spirituality may temporarily disguise itself, but hypocrisy can't be hidden forever. When you're having conversations, listen closely for sincerity over superficiality, depth over dogma. Are they judgmental, selfish, or materialistic? Are their morals flexible? Did they tell you they were okay with waiting until marriage but then tried to sleep with you the first time y'all were alone? Pay attention to inconsistencies between their claims and conduct. Actions reflect priorities. Let those speak louder than learned religious phrases.

Basing your relationship on external indicators of faith alone is a dangerous gamble. You risk being deceived, disappointed, or disillusioned. You may end up with someone who not only doesn't truly love Jesus, which causes you two to be unequally yoked. This might drag you down, hold you back, and pull you away from your destiny. Whoever he or she is, do you really think they're worth this risk?

While choosing to accept Christ is a one-time decision, choosing to live for Christ is a daily decision, and sometimes a minute-by-minute decision. If you're serious about your faith then you know how central it is to your identity, your core, your being, your sense of purpose. It informs your micro-decisions. How can you be with a person who doesn't identify with this pivotal part of your life? How can anything else matter more? Does it matter what else you have in common if you don't have the commonality of Christianity?

Agree To Disagree? Not On Jesus

Think about it. Life is a trip at times when you're by yourself, even with Jesus. How in the heck are you going to survive without Him at the center of your relationship, especially when you add another person's personality, issues, concerns, needs, desires, habits, flaws, and sinful nature to your own? You may not have everything in common and that's fine, but if you don't agree on Jesus, aren't you baiting major issues?

HAVE THE JESUS TALK

Amos 3:3 (NLT) Can two people walk together without agreeing on the direction?

Flirt To Convert? Let's Talk About Evangelistic Dating

The soil is most fertile for a rich relationship when both parties are on a similar spiritual level, and both are interested in growing together in Christ. When you date with the primary purpose of leading someone to Christ, it's called *evangelistic dating*.

If you meet someone who's attractive with a pleasant disposition and warm spirit, and you get the sense that they're a kindhearted person but they aren't saved, I won't tell you that they're not worth giving it a shot. It could be that God meant for you to meet so that you could introduce them to Christ, no matter their previous exposure to a godly upbringing.

But, and this is a big *but*, if you're going to go this route, you have to immediately start talking to them about Christ. And I mean from the moment you find out that they don't know Jesus.

Make it clear that while you're interested in the possibility of going out, they'll need to visit your church a few times, and then you can see where things go from there. Invite them to connect with your church on social media, so they can see what your church is about.

Sometimes, well, a lot of times, the conversation will end there. The reality is, Christians and non-Christians have different agendas, different objectives when it comes to lifestyle choices, and very little in common when it comes to life, period. This is not a condemnation of unbelievers, but rather an important distinction to emphasize exactly why believers and unbelievers don't mesh well as a couple.

However, if the conversation doesn't end as soon as you invite them to church and they express interest in wanting to know more about your beliefs, by all means, share the Gospel of Jesus Christ with them. Your divine commission as a witness for Christ is to evangelize the unsaved. Dating is a secondary aim if the opportunity to get someone saved presents itself.

Admittedly, I do have people in my church who hooked up with people who were not believers when they met, but the unbelieving person saw Christ in the person who was a believer, was won over to the Lord's side, and has never looked back.

Again, I do not believe this is a useful posture to have when dating. I don't think you should even give yourself the false hope of believing that one day, because a person appears to have a good heart, that they'll give it to the Lord, and to you too.

If it happens, it's a twofold blessing to be sure. But, if your heart is set on the person being your soulmate from the beginning, you are setting yourself up for clouded judgment later, when you'll need to be able to see objectively. Your motives, when bringing an unbeliever to the Lord, need to be grounded in your desire to see the person saved from a future of eternal damnation, not your desire to see them in your future.

Even if you do convince them to come to church and they make the choice to accept Jesus Christ as their personal savior, determining their sincerity will take time. Pastor Mike Todd says in his book, *Relationship Goals*, you marry patterns, not potential. You can't prove how much you love Christ and how committed you are to the cause of Christianity in only a month.

I have had men in my church go through six months of new members classes, small groups, and any other prerequisite for getting involved in ministry, just to win the affection of a spiritually mature young woman only to reveal later that he only wanted her, not Christ. Of course, by that time, if she wasn't vigilant and attentive in her observation of his motives and behavior, she fell for him and was emotionally wrecked when she found out his faith was fraudulent.

The Challenges Of Evangelistic Dating

While it can work, evangelistic dating is certainly not the most constructive way to date. To wit, there are fundamental flaws in this approach, the most glaring of which is the fact that you're starting your courtship by trying to get a person to change. That's not a promising idea.

Now, you *might* convince them to change. Or, if you can get them in front of a good Bible-teaching pastor, he may say something that moves them toward Christ, and they are inspired to change as a result. This has certainly happened at The Word Church.

Plenty of women have brought men who were interested in them to our church with the hopes that I would say something these men could relate to. The relationships didn't always work, but in many cases, the woman's evangelistic efforts did. The man did end up getting saved and joining our church.

But again, there's a much better way. I believe you should wait and believe God for someone who is already saved, especially if you've been with God for a while and you consider yourself to be spiritually mature.

I can't tell you all the horror stories my wife and I have heard over the years from in our church that made the choice to marry an unbeliever and are dealing with the regrettable consequences of living with someone day after day who has no fear and reverence for God.

Try to date someone who not only loves Jesus but loves Him more than you. You both might love Jesus so much that you try to out-do each other in loving Him. This is definitely preferable to trying to convince someone of *why* they should love Jesus.

Set A Timeline For Conversion

If you go the way of evangelistic dating, one of the things you must figure out quickly is how long you're going to give this person to figure out if they want to be saved. Keep in mind that the decision to accept Christ is a deeply personal one, and you're not the salvation police. It's not your job to decide when a person should give their life to Christ, but it is your job to decide how long you will wait for them to do so before you move on.

You also don't want to get caught up in a situation you shouldn't be in because even though you're spirit-filled, you're a spirit-filled human with very real human emotions. You get lonely, you get weak, you get tempted. You only entertained them in the first place because they had other great qualities that made you overlook that one enormous red flag. And now, it's been a while since you've had the company of a companion. You haven't had sex in like, years. They always smell good. They always look good. They always make you laugh. They always listen...

Don't give yourself too much credit. Being overly confident when you're dating someone who doesn't have Christ will get you into a world of trouble. You remember what Paul says in 1 Corinthians 10:12 (NLT), don't you? "If you think you're standing strong, be careful not to fall."

The longer you stay, the deeper your attraction will go. Then one day, you'll look up and realize that you're in love with someone who doesn't love Jesus and may not ever love Him. Now, you're faced with a heartrending decision that never had to be. Or worse yet, a wonderful moment turns to weakness, you have sex, and just like that, six years of celibacy and waiting for the right one is right out of the window. And all for someone who doesn't love Jesus.

Is this really how you want to do this?

The Perils Of Spiritual Incompatibility

Let's say you have Jesus in common at a very basic level. That's good. Now, let's say you always wanted a spouse who would pray for and speak life over you. That's good too if you're willing to do the same.

It may be difficult to demand that someone pour into you spiritually everyday if you are unwilling or unable to reciprocate. I don't know if it's fair to require a mate to pray for you on a regular basis, when it's been so long since you and God talked that you feel uncomfortable whenever you're asked to pray. You might be codependent, looking for someone to make up for what you lack spiritually, or worse, looking for someone to save you. Nah, that's now how it's supposed to work either.

Further, when one person is considerably more interested in spiritual matters than the other, tension or frustration may drive a wedge between you. One person may crave mutual intimacy with God through prayer or study while the other remains complacent or distant.

One may want to engage in thoughtful theological discussions based on a new book that they're reading while the other is averse to these kinds of conversations and satisfied with keeping things surface-level. A person's spiritual incompetence can be disappointing in times when you need insight or when you want to have a conversation about spiritual matters.

If you're comfortable where you are spiritually and don't see the need to deepen your relationship with Christ any further, then you probably aren't going to be happy with the person who is constantly pursuing ways to experience more of the fullness of God. You may become annoyed or resistant if the person asks you to fast, pray, and seek God with them for deeper revelation about a situation they're going through, if you consider spending time with God to be something reserved for weekends.

Or perhaps you do feel you should be spending more time with God, but at this time, your convictions aren't strong enough to inspire you to change. If someone tries to encourage that change before you are ready, you'll resent them for it. It may even feel like they don't love you for who you are.

If you're not synced in shared conviction, it's easy to experience friction, or perhaps worse, drift apart. For all these reasons and more, you need to have The Jesus Talk with your potential partner because when you're choosing a mate, your goals should be spiritually analogous. You should be clear about each other's spiritual ambition or ambivalence to avoid feelings of dissatisfaction surfacing later.

Accepting Differences In Spiritual Maturity

Based on what I've experienced, I can't in good conscience, say that two people with varying levels of spirituality can't have a meaningful relationship. It is possible to be content with someone who is more or less spiritual than you, if you realize what implications this can and will have on your relationship.

Your future mate may not be the person you have deep theological discussions with; however, he or she may be able to listen to you talk about it for hours, intrigued by your passion for God, and that may be enough.

Conversely, if you're not exactly a biblical scholar but you desire to learn more about Christ, then a person with a higher spiritual education than you may be quite attractive. A connection like this one could be replete with opportunities for the two of you to grow in God's word together. Perhaps they have the spirit of a teacher and you have the heart of a student.

You too, should be in love with Jesus. Knowing Him personally will give you an indispensable edge in dating and you want that advantage. There are so many people with their own goals in mind when they approach you, and many times, those goals won't include a long-term, loving, holy relationship. Unfortunately, especially for women who want to love and be loved, it's not always easy to detect what a person's objectives are at the onset.

However, when you have a relationship with Christ, He'll talk to you, and without sin blocking your ability to hear clearly, you'll be able to discern the motives of those with impure intentions and make sensible decisions long before you've taken any emotional risks.

Being in tune with the Holy Spirit can save you considerable time, effort, and energy, and eliminate the possibility of weeks, months, and even years laden with confusion, frustration, and disappointment.

Before you begin a relationship with anyone, I would strongly recommend taking inventory of your relationship with Christ, and evaluating where you are in your faith. Whatever that level is, that's the degree to which you are going to be successful in your relationship with a human being. The stronger your relationship with Christ, the better chances you have at selecting the mate He would have you to be with and the more likely you are to experience joy and satisfaction in a relationship that will ultimately lead to marriage.

The Lifeline Of Deep Shared Faith

Now, if you find someone who has a deep and personal relationship with Jesus Christ, you may have found a treasure. If they check all those other boxes, feel free to proceed. A deep shared faith is a priceless gift and protective shield. It doesn't mean you won't have to go through some stuff. It means that when those storms come in mighty and fast, your faith will be the rope that ties you both to the Rock of Ages.

With Christ at the center, spiritual intimacy reinforces emotional intimacy. It provides a wellspring of wisdom and grace to weather challenges as a team. When you have a partner who loves you and who loves Jesus more than you, that shared faith is your lifeline, and it nourishes your relationship in ways that nothing else can.

The Blessings And Benefits Of Shared Faith

- **Same foundation, same destination.** Sharing deep faith means you both have a similar outlook on what's important in life and where you want to go together. This makes decisions easier and minimizes arguments... ahem, heated fellowship.

- **You'll really get each other.** You and your partner will have a deeper insight into each other's values, fears, hopes, and motivations. You'll communicate more effectively, listen more attentively, and empathize more compassionately. You'll connect more emotionally, mentally, and spiritually.

- **You'll bounce back faster.** Together, you'll find strength in tough times, tapping into your faith for support. This means you worry less, lean on each other more, and get through the hard stuff together.

- **Raising the bar.** Expecting more from each other in line with your shared faith means you'll work harder to honor, forgive, and grow together. It's like having a built-in accountability partner. It keeps things in high gear.

- **Amplified Impact and Influence:** Your relationship becomes more than just "you and me." Together, you're a powerhouse duo with the potential to bring about real change. You have a shared purpose and a deeper desire to serve God and others. You become a team that's not only good for each other, but good for everyone around you.

These aren't just feel-good promises; they're real and lasting benefits grounded in God's word and power. If the person you choose to partner with matches your faith walk, you can create a meaningful and influential bond that can withstand the challenges and changes of life. No, spiritual compatibility is not a miraculous solution that will solve every problem you'll ever face, but in a world of uncertainties and adversity, spiritual compatibility can provide you with a level of steadiness, comfort, and stability.

RULE 6
KNOW WHAT DIRECTION YOU'RE DATING IN

(DIRECTIONAL DATING)

"The heart wants what it wants, but the spirit knows what it needs. Seek God's direction in your dating. He'll never steer you wrong." -*Dr. R. A. Vernon*

As important as it is to have Christ in common as a couple, it's not enough. When you're looking for a life partner, you need someone who can engage with you on a multitude of topics; someone whose attractiveness is more than skin deep because let's face it, beauty fades, bodies age, and we all need substance to carry us through. This brings us to the concept of directional dating.

Date In The Right Direction

When you hear the term 'directional dating,' you might think it's simply about ensuring that you and your partner are on the same page, heading towards a shared future. And while that's certainly part of it, I want to challenge you to think bigger. It's not only about both of you moving forward together; it's also about understanding where each of you started and how that affects where you're headed. It's about looking at the whole map of your lives, not just the destination you're aiming for.

In the mating dance, as in life, you're moving in one of three directions: up, down, or laterally. And let me be crystal clear - the direction you're headed matters big time. This trajectory not only shapes your shared experiences and relationship outcomes, but also the roles you naturally assume within your relationship over time.

We're talking who takes the lead and who follows, who has the final say on decisions, and whose ambitions take priority when you're making major moves. Your direction can determine whether you're ego-tripping teammates constantly vying for position or a power couple firing on all cylinders, where leadership and support roles interchange fluidly based on context, not control.

From Longwood To Love

As we talk about these directional dynamics, let me share a bit of my own journey. I'm from the Longwood projects of Cleveland, where hope was as thin as the walls and dreams were deferred daily. I've seen days when the fridge was emptier than a promise from a politician, as my early years were steeped in poverty—a reality that taught me the value of grit and the taste of hope. The roach-infested apartments I called home and the pangs of hunger that often visited were my daily companions. Yet, it was there, among the struggle and the scarcity, that I decided that my start didn't have to determine my finish.

My wife, Victory, on the other hand, grew up in a very different environment. Her childhood was painted with broader strokes of security and stability, the kind of comfort that was foreign to my childhood. Her family wasn't wealthy, but they lived in a neighborhood where the lawns were manicured and the future seemed as bright as the streetlights that lit up their clean, tree-lined streets. For her, safety was a given, not a privilege.

She never knew the kind of hunger that gnawed at your belly or the kind of cold that seeped into your bones when in a house with no heat. As the baby of the family and a preacher's kid, her struggles were real, but different. For her, it was never about survival; it was about figuring out who she was under the watchful eyes of a whole congregation and carving out her own identity in a world that seemed to have it mapped out for her.

Victory's Path From Pastor's Kid To Pastor's Wife

Growing up as the daughter of a pastor, Victory had a front-row seat to the ins and outs of ministry life. She watched her mother hold it down as the consummate first lady with her grace and poise, always on point with a warm smile and an encouraging word, even when the weight of the congregation's needs pressed heavy on her shoulders. Victory saw firsthand the delicate balance of being a public figure while trying to maintain a private family life, of being held to a higher standard while still being human.

That kind of pressure cooks up a special kind of patience, the kind you can't rush. And that patience? It was exactly what someone like me needed. Little did she know that these early experiences were preparing her for the role she would later assume as my wife and first lady. The lessons she learned from watching her mother - the importance of presenting a united front, of always being ready to serve, of maintaining grace under pressure - would become invaluable as she was cast into the spotlight by my side.

Raised in the shadow of the pulpit, Victory understood the assignment of being in leadership beside me and had a deep reservoir of faith and resilience to draw from. In a sense, her formative experience had prepared her for the form of dating up that came with becoming the wife of a pastor whose career was on the rise. The intrinsic muscle memory from her upbringing made her the perfect partner to walk with me in leading our flock.

Complementary Strengths: The Beauty Of Balance

In Victory, I found a partner who embodied the patience and emotional steadiness that I respected and needed to grow in myself. Her ability to remain grounded and even keeled in the face of challenges is a source of inspiration and balance for me. This dynamic is a powerful reminder that dating up isn't always about external markers of success or status; it can also be about seeking out people who have the qualities we need to develop in ourselves. By being open to learning from Victory's emotional maturity, I found myself growing in ways that not only made me a better husband, but a better leader and person.

At the same time, my drive and enthusiasm beautifully complemented Victory's patience and steadiness. My strong will and high energy brought a sense of momentum and excitement to our partnership, while her calm demeanor grounded us and kept us steady. In this way, our contrasting qualities became a source of stability, each of us dating up in the ways we needed to increase.

The Influence Of Our Origins

Our story is evidence of how our pasts can influence our dating direction in both overt and subtle ways. Victory's experiences growing up had set her on a path that made stepping into the role of first lady a natural fit, even if it wasn't a conscious or calculated choice. And for me, dating someone with her level of emotional maturity and relational intelligence was a form of dating up that challenged me to step up in ways that required me to evolve, stimulating immense personal growth while enhancing our togetherness.

By the time our lives intertwined romantically, I was a long way from Longwood, but this juxtaposition of our beginnings could easily have been a barrier between us. Instead, it became our bridge. Victory brought a sense of peace and possibility into my world that I hadn't known growing up, while I shared with her the resilience and unrelenting drive that had propelled me out of the projects. Our directional dating journey wasn't just about finding common ground; it was about envisioning the ground we could cover together, with her gifts complementing my weaknesses, and mine, hers.

For us, we found that the power of directional dating was not in erasing our differences or pretending that they didn't exist, but in leveraging them in a way that honored our pasts and our future. It's a reminder that God uses every part of our story—every struggle, every lesson, every experience—to shape us for the calling He has placed on our lives.

From Different Paths To A Shared Destiny

Getting to this point didn't happen overnight. It took real talk, understanding, and a willingness to see the world through each other's eyes. By doing the work, we found our shared path—a journey that led us to where we are today.

Our story is just one example of how coming from different backgrounds can be a powerful testament to the depth and resilience possible in a relationship. It also shows how our origins can influence the direction we date and lead us to unexpected places of growth and fulfillment.

If you had told me back in my Longwood days that I'd one day be a pastor with a wife who was the perfect embodiment of a first lady, I would've laughed. And if you had told Victory that her upbringing as a preacher's kid was preparing her to be the partner and first lady to someone from my neck of the woods, she probably would've been just as skeptical.

But by being open to dating outside our comfort zones and trusting that our experiences have prepared us for the journey, we can find ourselves in partnerships and roles that push us to be our best selves. Victory and I are living proof of this. Our directional dating journey brought us together not just as partners, but as a team working towards a calling that was beyond our wildest dreams.

The Art Of Directional Dating: Finding Your Way In Love

Let's break down and define what it really means to date up, down, or laterally. Each direction comes with its own set of experiences and potential difficulties that you need to navigate with wisdom and foresight to give your relationship a chance to flourish. You also need to have the self-awareness to know why you date in the direction you do, as we sometimes have blind spots or hidden motivations born from our past wounds or unfulfilled desires.

Of course, sometimes people date with no conscious thought of the direction because they've found someone they connect with, regardless of their background or status. They simply do not care what a person has or doesn't have, as it has no bearing on what they feel for them.

Dating Up: The Allure And The Challenge

When you date up, you're dating someone whose life experiences, accomplishments, or resources are perceived as superior to your own in some way. This might mean they have a more prestigious job, higher education level, come from a wealthier background, or have stronger spiritual maturity. Dating up can be both intimidating and inspiring. It can open your eyes to new possibilities and ways of living. It can challenge you to strive for improvement in your own life and generate a sense of aspiration, but it's not without its challenges.

It can stir up feelings of inadequacy or create pressure to keep up. You might grapple with feeling like you don't quite belong, with the nagging anxiety that you have to prove your worth or to fit into a world that feels unfamiliar. It's not uncommon to confront subtle (or not-so-subtle) power imbalances or to find yourself fighting to preserve your sense of identity. Be careful here, as you don't want to end up feeling like you're competing with your partner rather than complementing them.

So why do we sometimes seek out partners who are above us in some way? Is it simply because we are attracted to success and status? Or is there something deeper at play?

There's no single answer to these questions people have their own individual reasons for dating up. But here are a few potential factors that may contribute to this dynamic:

- **We're magnetized by ambition and drive.** People who have achieved a high level of success often possess qualities like ambition, determination, and drive that can be incredibly attractive. For some, this attraction might stem from the intoxicating inspiration that comes from witnessing another's tenacious dedication towards their goals.

- **The natural human desire for growth and improvement.** We're wired to be attracted to those who we think can help us attain a better life. It could be that we are seeking validation or affirmation, or trying to fill a void within ourselves that we believe can be filled by someone we view as superior.

- **We yearn for what we lack.** At times, we find ourselves inexplicably drawn towards partners whose backgrounds or lifestyles starkly contrast with our own because it piques our curiosity. We might be pulled in by the tantalizing promise of a life we've never known or an unconscious craving for some excitement and novelty in our dating lives.

Dating Down: The Appeal And The Peril

Conversely, when you date down, you are in a relationship with someone whose life experiences, accomplishments, or resources are perceived as subordinate to your own. They may have attained less education, come from less affluent backgrounds, or be less mature spiritually or otherwise.

Just like dating up, there can be both positive and negative aspects to dating down. It's important to understand why we may be drawn towards partners who are deemed "less successful" by certain standards and the potential challenges that come with it. You might find yourself feeling like you need to 'save' or 'fix' your partner, or that you're constantly having to lower your standards or expectations.

So why do people choose to date down? Here are some possible reasons:

- **To feel needed and valued.** When you're the one with more resources or life experience, it can be gratifying to feel needed and appreciated. You might enjoy being the one who can provide guidance, support, and stability.

- **To assert control and power.** In some cases, dating down can be a way to assert control in a relationship. If you're the one with more power and influence, you might feel more secure and in charge.

- **Fear of rejection or abandonment.** Sometimes, dating someone we perceive to be 'beneath' us is driven by insecurities or fear of rejection. We may believe a person will be less likely to abandon us or undermine our confidence, which can seem like a protective strategy, but it risks undervaluing both partners in the long term.

- **Impaired view of self-worth.** Some individuals see themselves as less successful or desirable than they truly are and unknowingly settle for less in their relationships. They have an underlying belief that they are undeserving of more. In this case, they may not necessarily feel like they're dating down because they're oblivious to the discrepancy between their qualities and those of their partner.

- **The joy of nurturing.** Some people derive great joy and satisfaction from being in a nurturing role within their relationships. They appreciate the opportunity to support and encourage their partner's growth and achievements, finding fulfillment in their partner's successes and gratitude.

Dating Laterally: A Level Playing Field

Dating laterally is often seen as the safe choice, where you and your partner have similar life experiences, accomplishments, or resources. It could mean sharing the same educational background, socio-economic class, or level of spiritual maturity. This type of dating can feel comfortable and reassuring, like coming home to who truly gets the world you come from because they come from it too.

When you're on equal footing, it can alleviate some of the power struggles or insecurities that crop up when dating up or down. There's

KNOW WHAT DIRECTION YOU'RE DATING IN

a natural ease when you're with someone operating at your level. This can be comforting for sure, but just because it feels comfortable doesn't mean it's always the best move. Like the other dating directions, this too has its pros and cons. If things come too easily, you may become complacent. Additionally, if you both have weaknesses in the same areas, they may be amplified when together.

So why do folks tend to date laterally? Let's look at a few reasons:

- **Similar values and interests**. There's something to be said about the ease that comes with dating someone who just gets it. Connecting with people who are on the same wavelength in terms of values, goals, and interests can make you feel seen and understood on a whole 'nother level.

- **Comfort in familiarity.** We are creatures of habit, after all. There's a certain comfort in sticking with what we know and staying in our lane. Dating someone from a similar background or station in life can feel safe and easy because it's familiar territory. You likely have comparable lifestyles and ways of seeing and moving through the world. No navigating unchartered waters. No intimidating unfamiliar ground.

- **Fear of being "too much" or "not enough."** Some people might choose to date laterally out of fear. They worry that if they date up, they may not measure up to their partner's expectations or that if they date down, they may compromise their own standards and expectations.

- **To avoid power imbalances.** Lateral dating minimizes a lot of the power dynamics that can pop up from dating up or down. With neither person coming from a place of superiority, you have the chance to build an equal partnership from the jump. Shared values and visions for the future can develop organically and smoothly.

Now, let's pause for a moment and take a bird's eye view of what we've just unpacked. We've explored the ins and outs of dating up, down, and laterally—the good, the bad, and the sometimes complicated. To help you visualize these concepts side by side, I've put together a handy chart for you.

Navigating The Directions Of Dating: A Comparative Overview

DATING UP

Examples	Pros
Your partner might have a more decorated academic background, hold a high-ranking professional role, or hail from an affluent lineage.	Access to broader life experiences. Motivation for self enhancement. Aspirations ignited by partner's drive.

Cons	Strategies
Inner struggle with self-worth. Strain from attempting to match their pace. Navigating the dynamic of unequal footing.	Celebrate and leverage differences. Foster a shared vision for the future. Prioritize communication to bridge gaps. Champion mutual respect and support.

KNOW WHAT DIRECTION YOU'RE DATING IN

DATING DOWN

Examples	Pros
Engaging with a partner who might not have pursued higher education or who comes from a more modest upbringing.	Fulfillment from being a supportive cornerstone. Gratification from being deeply appreciated. Potential to lead and guide the relationship's direction.
Cons	**Strategies**
Risk of fostering dependency. Emotional drain from overextending oneself. Possible feelings of imbalance in contribution.	Encourage partner's self-reliance and goals. Establish boundaries to prevent codependency. Recognize and celebrate your partner's intrinsic qualities.

DATING LATERALLY

Examples	Pros
Pairing with someone who mirrors your own educational achievements, socioeconomic status, or spiritual journey.	Shared understanding of life experiences. Natural alignment of ambitions and life views. Equal contributions to the relationship.

Cons	Strategies
Possibility of mutual stagnation. Challenges when both have similar blind spots. Less impetus for individual growth.	Cultivate personal passions alongside the relationship. Adopt a growth mindset to inspire joint self-improvement. Introduce diverse activities to stimulate personal and relational development.

Bringing Consciousness To Your Choices

No matter which direction you tend to date, the crucial point here is to bring consciousness into your choices and ensure that these are driven by healthful motivations rather than hidden insecurities or fears. The truth of the matter is, life happens, and at any time, there could be a shift in any of our stations in life. While one partner may be in a more successful or accomplished position today, tomorrow their circumstances could change. An illness, a job loss, an unexpected windfall—all have the power to shake up the dynamics and turn the tables.

The question then, isn't necessarily whether we should always strive to date up or avoid dating down. It's more about being intentional with our choices, considering why we lean towards certain partners, and ensuring that we're motivated by a heart that seeks God's will above all, ensuring that our romantic choices honor Him and reflect our commitment to living out our faith in every aspect of our lives.

Watch Out When All Your Arrows Are Pointing South

We've established that each dating direction has advantages and disadvantages, but there's one scenario where extreme caution is warranted: when you find yourself dating down in every area. This is when your partner is not just from a less privileged background or has accumulated or achieved less in life than you have, but also lacks that burning desire to keep climbing, that unrelenting drive for self-improvement that you possess. In this situation, the potential for stagnation and resentment is heightened.

When you're dating down in every area, you might find yourself constantly feeling like you're carrying the weight of the relationship. When you're the one always pushing for progress, always trying to hype your partner up, always having to temper your expectations because your partner can't handle your go-getter mentality, that's a lot. Over time, this can trigger frustration, wear you down, and make you feel like you're stuck in neutral.

Plus, you don't want to slip into that hero role (the "savior complex"), like it's your responsibility to 'fix' your partner, their circumstances, or their whole life. That's not a relationship; that's a project. You'll be out here emotionally taxed, playing Captain Save-a-boo, and that's not the move. Before you know it, you're entangled in a codependent situation where your sense of worth is tied to your ability to rescue or level up your partner. This is an exhausting cycle and will eventually drain you.

Not only that, but if you're always the one behind the wheel, it's tough for your partner to find their own drive or even believe they're capable of driving. They might start over-relying on you, and before you know it, they're not even trying to level up. That's not healthy for either of you and it will lead to an increasingly lopsided relationship.

Now, let me be clear. This isn't about judging someone's worth based on their background or current circumstances. Everyone has value, period. But in a relationship, both partners need to be about that refusal to become complacent and put in work for the partnership. If you're the one always pulling and your partner is always getting dragged, then I hate to be the one to break it to you... no, actually, I'm happy to be the one to break it to you: You're playing yourself.

Dating Downhill: Is The Slide Worth The Ride?

If this sounds like the situation you're in right now, it's time to put everything on the table. Have a real talk with your partner. Let them know what you're feeling and that you want a relationship where both of you are actively invested. They have to come up with their own goals and chase them with that same energy.

But also, keep it 100 with yourself. If your partner isn't trying to match your hustle or invest in the relationship the way you do, you might have to think about whether y'all are really clicking. It's not selfish to want a partner who challenges you, supports your growth, and brings something to the table. In fact, it's necessary for a relationship that's actually going somewhere.

Remember, a relationship should lift you up, not weigh you down. Every couple has stuff to work through, but when you're dating down

KNOW WHAT DIRECTION YOU'RE DATING IN

in every area, you're signing up for a unique set of difficulties that can be hard to overcome without a strong commitment from both partners and a radical shift in mindset from at least one.

I know it's not easy to leave when you care about someone. Your big heart wants to keep pouring love into them, hoping they'll rise up. I get it. But here's the tea—you can't fill a cup that has holes in it, and as the saying goes, "You can't light yourself on fire to keep someone else warm." If you are intent on staying, however, I need you to revisit Rule 3, specifically, the parable of the pitcher and the cup.

STRATEGIC NAVIGATION IN DIRECTIONAL DATING

Now that we've discussed the benefits, drawbacks, and dynamics of dating up, down, and laterally, let's talk strategy. Maybe you're looking up at your partner, or perhaps they're looking up at you. Or maybe you're seeing eye-to-eye, but you're coming from different worlds. How can you date in the direction that sets your relationship up for success? Consider the following suggestions.

Communicate Like Your Love Life Depends On It

Because, guess what? It does. When it comes to backgrounds, where you are currently, and where you want to go, talk about it. If you've got more degrees than a thermometer but your partner barely made it out of high school, don't dance around it. Tackle what that mix means for the two of you head on, because it will mean something.

Perhaps it means that you'll be the primary breadwinner of the family, while they happily manage the home and the kids. Or maybe it means they'll return to school while you support them on that journey. Whatever it is—address it, don't suppress it. Honest communication brings clarity to a cloudy situation and can act as your GPS in the relationship.

Balance The Power To Create A More Equal Partnership

This is especially important if you're dating up or down. When one partner has more resources, more influence, more social capital, it can be easy for the other partner to feel like they're constantly playing catch-up or like their contributions aren't as valuable. That's not okay. You both need to feel like you're on equal footing. This might mean evaluating and adjusting how decision-making processes are handled in the relationship. Ensure that both partners have an equal say in choices that affect you both, from minor decisions like choosing a movie to significant ones like financial planning.

It might also mean being intentional about how you introduce each other to friends and family, about how you navigate social situations where one of you might feel out of place. The key is to be proactive in addressing these imbalances and finding ways to create a more equitable dynamic. Support each other, lift each other up, and make sure neither of you feels overshadowed or underappreciated.

Maintain Your Individual Identity And Encourage Your Partner To Do The Same

Never forget who you are. Remember that person you were before you got into a relationship? They're still there, and they still matter. Make sure you're carving out time for your own interests and goals. And make sure your partner is doing the same. You both need to have space to pursue your individual goals, to challenge yourselves and each other. A relationship is about sharing lives, not giving them up. Keep your own hobbies, your own friends, and your own time. This isn't just good for you; it's good for your relationship too. It keeps things fresh and gives you both something to talk about besides what's for dinner.

Support Each Other's Growth

Creating an equal partnership isn't just about balancing power; it's also about supporting each other's growth. When you're in a directional dating situation it can be easy to fall into a mentor-mentee dynamic, where one partner is always teaching and the other is always learning. Growth should not be one-sided, with one partner constantly pushing the other to improve while remaining stagnant themselves. Instead, both individuals should be committed to evolving together, encouraging and challenging each other to become the best versions of themselves.

This might mean taking turns pursuing educational or career goals, with one partner taking the lead while the other offers support and encouragement, and then switching roles when the time is right. It could also involve setting shared goals for personal development, such as learning a new skill together or pushing each other to do something that requires an increased level of faith and self-belief.

Remember, growth is not just about achieving external milestones; it's also about developing emotional intelligence, communication skills, and self-awareness. Make a habit of checking in with each other about your personal development journey, celebrating each other's progress, and offering gentle, constructive feedback when necessary. When you both prioritize growth, you create a relationship that is dynamic, fulfilling, and continually evolving.

Your Relationship, Your Rules

Dealing with the chatter of external judgments about your relationship can be straight-up stressful. Y'all know what I'm talking about.

Friends, family, and sometimes even strangers will have something to say about who you should be dating. "Oh, they're not on your level." "They're way too *this*." "They're not enough *that*." It's like everyone's got an opinion, but the only two that really matter are yours and your partner's. Stay true to what you know about each other, not what others think they know about you. Your relationship isn't a democracy; it's not up for public voting.

At the same time, don't cut off a source of wisdom or guidance entirely. Just because Auntie Sharon can't stop comparing your love life to her favorite soap opera doesn't mean she doesn't know what she's talking about. If a trusted advisor tells you ol' boy or ol' girl isn't good for you, it's worth taking a pause and evaluating their advice. Auntie may be a little too into her stories, but she's also seen a few more years than you.

Discernment is key here. Know when to nod and smile, and when to really listen. Take the advice that aligns with God's word and your personal convictions and tune out the rest.

Beware Of Background Bias: Privilege Doesn't Define Potential

Finally, and this is a big one, don't let your partner's background or circumstances completely define them or limit your perception of their potential. While it's true that our pasts shape us and our patterns matter, it's also important to recognize that growth and change are possible. Just because someone comes from a less privileged background doesn't automatically mean they're less intelligent, less capable, or less ambitious.

And just because someone comes from a more privileged background doesn't necessarily mean they're more sophisticated, more worldly, or more successful. These are stereotypes, and while they may hold kernels of truth for some individuals, they shouldn't be the sole basis for judging someone's worth or potential in a healthy, respectful relationship.

See your partner for who they are, not just where they come from. Take the time to understand how their background has influenced them, but also recognize their individuality and capacity for growth. Believe in their potential, while also being mindful of their past. Encourage them to break free from negative patterns and to develop new, positive ones. When they doubt themselves, when they feel like they don't belong or they're not good enough, be there to remind them of their worth, their brilliance, and their possibility for growth.

Your partner's background may influence their destiny, but it is their faith, their actions, and their willingness to grow that will ultimately determine it.

God is in the business of transformation, remember? He took a shepherd boy and made him a king (David), turned a stutterer into a spokesman (Moses), and a prostitute into a protector (Rahab). He can certainly work wonders with you and the person you're dating.

Enjoy The Journey

Navigating the twists and turns of directional dating isn't easy, but by communicating openly, supporting each other's growth, and seeing each other's potential, you can build a relationship that transcends direction and defies expectation. With God as your guide and your partner by your side, there's no limit to how high you can go. Just remember to enjoy the view along the way.

When Directional Dating Becomes A Deal-Breaker

Now, I know we've been talking about directional dating and how to make it work, but sometimes, the directional difference is just too great to overcome. Sometimes, despite your best efforts, you find yourself in a relationship that's taxing you in every way. That's when you need to know when to say, "enough is enough," and walk away.

So, how do you know when a directional difference is too much? Well, there are a few key signs to look out for.

First, if you find yourself constantly compromising your own values, goals, or beliefs to accommodate your partner's, that's a red flag. If you're feeling more drained than a smartphone at the end of a long day, it's a sign. If you're always the one bending, always the one sacrificing, always the one putting your dreams on hold, something's got to give.

Second, if your partner consistently dismisses or undermines your experiences, your perspective, or your feelings, that's another warning sign. If they're always pulling the "well, in my world" card, making you feel like your reality is invalid, or gaslighting you, you need to know that this kind of behavior reveals a self-centered partner who lacks the emotional intelligence for a healthy relationship. Your thoughts, ideas, and feelings matter, and your partner should respect them.

Finally, if you've tried to address the directional difference, if you've communicated openly and honestly, if you've sought help and guidance, and you're still not making progress, it might be time to accept that the gap is too wide. It's not about failure; it's about recognizing when something isn't working and having the courage to make a change.

Once you've identified that the directional difference is too great, trust your instincts and move on. Leaving someone you care about is never easy, but sometimes, it's the most loving thing you can do, both for yourself and for your partner.

Remember, you are not responsible for your partner's growth or happiness, but you are responsible for yours. You can support them, encourage them, and love them, but ultimately, they are on their own journey. If that journey is no longer aligned with yours, if it's pulling you backwards instead of propelling you forward, it's okay to choose a different path.

Prioritizing your own well-being doesn't mean being selfish or disregarding your partner's needs. It means recognizing that you need to take care of yourself in order to be a good partner, a good friend, a good steward of your own life. It means setting healthy boundaries, advocating for your own needs, and being willing to make tough choices when necessary. At the end of the day, you are the only one who can live your life. You are the only one who can pursue your purpose, fulfill your potential, and answer to your Creator.

Don't let a directional difference derail you from your destiny.

Trust yourself, trust God, and trust the journey. If a relationship is no longer serving you, let it go, so you can make space for something better.

Learning And Growing From Directional Dating Experiences

Every relationship gives you some takeaways. Take some time to reflect on your past directional dating experiences. What worked well? What didn't? What patterns do you notice in the types of partners you're attracted to or the challenges you tend to face?

Maybe you've realized that you have a tendency to date up because you're drawn to ambition and success, but you often find yourself feeling inadequate or like you're constantly trying to prove yourself. Or maybe you've noticed that you tend to date down because you enjoy feeling needed and appreciated, but you often end up feeling drained and resentful.

Whatever your patterns are, take note of them. Don't judge yourself or beat yourself up but be honest about what you're noticing. These insights can be valuable clues about what you need in a partner, what you need to feel fulfilled in a relationship, and what areas you might need to work on in yourself.

Using Directional Dating Experiences As Opportunities For Personal Growth And Self-Discovery

Once you've reflected on your patterns and insights, use them as a springboard for personal growth and self-discovery. If you've realized that you tend to date up because you're seeking validation or status, take some time to work on your own self-esteem and sense of worth. Develop your own interests, pursue your own goals, and learn to validate yourself from the inside out.

If you've noticed that you tend to date down because you're afraid of being alone or you don't believe you deserve better, challenge those beliefs. Surround yourself with people who uplift and inspire you, and practice setting healthy boundaries in your relationships.

If you've learned that you need a partner who supports your growth and encourages you to pursue your dreams, make that a non-negotiable in your future relationships. If you've realized that you have a tendency to over-give and under-receive, do the work to figure out why, then do better going forward.

KNOW WHAT DIRECTION YOU'RE DATING IN

As we've covered in previous chapters, the more you work on your own personal development, the more equipped you'll be to navigate the ups and downs of dating and relationships. Take what you've learned, the good and the bad, and let it lead to some solid insight. Wrest wisdom from your failures. Turn every 'L' into a lesson. Use your revelations to make more informed choices about who you date and how you show up in your relationships.

Remember, the healthiest couples are those who've done the hard work of individual growth before attempting the joint journey of being one. Which leads perfectly into **Rule 7 | Discuss Each Other's Pasts**, because regardless of the direction in which you date, every relationship involves the merging of two separate histories, two unique narratives. The way forward is paved with truth-telling about where you've been - and that's our next critical discussion.

RULE 7
DISCUSS EACH OTHER'S PASTS

"The past is never where you think you left it." -*Katherine Anne Porter*

FROM FIRST DATE TO FULL DISCLOSURE

By this point in your dating journey, you should be pretty serious about the person you're dating. You've worked to become self-aware, you know your non-negotiables, you know not to ever negotiate your non-negotiables, you're clear on the fact that dating is an assignment, you've had The Jesus Talk, and you know what direction you're dating in. You're now ready to tackle another crucial topic: you and your partner's pasts.

DISCUSS EACH OTHER'S PASTS

When The Past Knocks, Who Will Answer—You Or Google?

In today's age of digital footprints and social media, it's becoming increasingly difficult to keep your past hidden. With social media as the new background check, damning screenshots acting as surprise witnesses in the courtroom of public opinion, and Google at everyone's fingertips, the reality is, we're all living in glass houses. Past relationships, questionable comments, and impulsive actions can be dug up with a few clicks and keystrokes.

With so much transparency, or perhaps overexposure, when it comes to discussing your past with a potential partner, it's not a matter of if, but when. The question is, will you control the narrative, or will they stumble upon it?

If there's something sensitive or potentially problematic from your past that may affect your relationship, it's better your partner hear it from you. Being upfront allows you to frame the discussion and prevents shocking revelations from blindsiding your partner and derailing your relationship. Talking about your past can feel uncomfortable, but it's necessary. This openness goes both ways.

There's no way you should consider marrying someone without thoroughly understanding their history. This would be like signing a permanent contract without reading the fine print – this isn't updating software or taking out a loan, this is your life.

You wouldn't buy a house without an inspection, so why commit to a lifetime partnership without one? And why would you expect someone to tie their future to yours without knowing exactly who or what they're binding themselves to?

That said, don't reveal your past to someone who will soon be a part of it. If you're on the fence about whether you have a future together, pump the brakes before you reveal anything too personal. If a person doesn't have the potential to be your spouse based on the first six rules, then why reveal the often painful, or if nothing else, private details of your life? Don't discuss your past relationships, home of origin issues, or anything else with someone unless they have passed the initial screening criteria.

If you believe this person is future spouse material, then it's time to get the lowdown on their background—their upbringing, exes, credit, job history, ongoing health issues—I'm talking full disclosure, the uncensored version of their autobiography.

The Past Ain't Just The Past

Everyone has a past that has sculpted them into who they are today. If you're serious about building something together, you need to understand each other's foundations before attempting to lay one together.

We've all heard it, "The past is in the past." But let's just park here for a moment and reflect on this statement. Is the past really in the past? Or is it more like an ever-present sleeping giant, easily awakened at the slightest provocation, demanding to be named and tamed? I think we all know the answer to that.

> **The idea that "the past is in the past" is convenient but inaccurate. Your past is a part of you as much as your present is.**

While you shouldn't be a prisoner of your past, if left unacknowledged and unprocessed, it can greatly impact your future decisions, reactions, and relationships.

Home Is Where the Heart (and Hurt) Is

Let's start with the basics: home of origin issues. The family you grew up in and the dynamics you witnessed and experienced have a signifi-

DISCUSS EACH OTHER'S PASTS

cant impact on how you approach relationships as an adult. Some key questions to consider:

- What was the family structure? Were there two biological parents in the home, or only one? Are their parents divorced? Were they ever married? Were they raised by a grandparent or foster parent?

- Did the parents have a healthy, God-honoring relationship?

- Was there open communication and healthy conflict resolution, or were problems swept under the rug?

- Was there any abuse, neglect, or trauma?

These experiences shape our attachment styles, our communication patterns, and our expectations for relationships. Someone who grew up in a home with a lot of conflict may have a higher tolerance for drama, while someone who grew up in a home where emotions were never discussed may struggle with vulnerability and emotional availability. If your partner grew up in a home where verbal disagreements were rare, they might avoid direct communication. If they had an absent or abusive father, they might have unresolved issues with trust or authority.

Now, having a challenging upbringing doesn't automatically disqualify someone from being a good partner, but it does mean that they need to have done the work to heal those early wounds. They need to have developed self-awareness about how their past impacts their present. And they need to be willing to continue that work within the context of your relationship.

If they deny that their upbringing had any effect on them, they lack self-awareness and likely have low emotional intelligence too. It's naïve to think that what we saw and experienced as a child won't have some bearing on our behavior as an adult, to say nothing of our conduct as a husband or wife.

The Impact Of Parental Relationships

To offer some more concrete examples, if the woman you're considering had the love of a godly father who prayed for, protected, and affirmed her all her life, in most cases, her expectations for you, whether she articulates them explicitly or not, are going to be different from a woman who was mistreated and neglected by her father.

If the man you like comes from a home where dad was missing and mom was unfit, how does he know how to love you properly? What model will he emulate? The lack of strong, healthy examples can leave someone fumbling in the dark as they try to navigate love and partnership.

No one is destined to repeat the mistakes of their parents but it takes conscious effort. If your potential partner isn't open about their past, or if they refuse to acknowledge its impact, that's a red flag that you shouldn't ignore.

How My Childhood Affected My Marriage

My own marriage exemplifies how home issues can play out. My parents were very young when they had me and being kids themselves, were unequipped to parent me in healthy ways. Consequently, when Victory and I first got married, I remember needing her to hold me often. It was deeper than desire. I longed for her to embrace me for hours at a time. It took me years to work through my past pain and realize that my need wasn't rooted in my affection for her, but rather the lack of affection I received as a child.

In the black context, we often talk about missing fathers, but please don't underestimate the effect a missing mother will have on a person as they get older, in particular, on a man. A man who is kissed, hugged, and loved on by his mother will not need the same things from his wife that a man who has mother-pain will.

If your future spouse did not receive something they needed as a child from either parent and they haven't worked through those issues, they will live in expectation for you to give it to them. It is an impossible standard for you to meet, but when you don't, it will compound their pain, and then cause a rift in your marriage.

The problem is, at that point, it becomes much harder to determine whether home of origin issues or new marital challenges are the root of the problem because it's easy to mask one issue with another once you get married. I told you it took years for me to figure out that my need for Lady Vernon to hold me wasn't about me connecting with her. It was about me connecting to the little boy from my past who needed his mother.

It was easy for me to assume that I just wanted to lay up under her because I loved the way it felt to be next to her. While that was and is true, I realized there was something unhealthy about it when I felt a deep sense of rejection when she wouldn't or couldn't hold me because she wanted or needed to do something else. No one likes to be refused an embrace, but the feeling I experienced was more intense. It was painful.

Navigating Tough Conversations

Considering what I've shared, pay close attention to your significant other's reactions when discussing their parents. Do they become tense or withdrawn at the mention of their father? Do they express resentment when their mother is brought up? Do they light up with joy when talking about their family, or do they seem distant and disconnected? Observe their responses carefully and don't hesitate to ask direct, thoughtful questions to better understand their relationship with their parents.

Don't skimp on this part of the conversation. Everything a person is in some way ties back to their view of and their relationship with their parents. Admittedly, this conversation is intrusive, but so what? Remember, you're on assignment. Be intentional and be selfish. Think about your feelings and future more than theirs because once you get married, you need to be selfless.

If at any point during your application of this rule you see or sense something shady, move on quickly, unless they agree to get help. If they refuse, welp, it was nice getting to know them, but you have no time for someone who isn't willing to confront their past and grow from it. Your future is far too valuable to get caught up in someone else's unresolved issues and there's no nobility in chaining yourself to a sinking ship.

Now, in all your being selfish, be sensitive. If you can tell a certain topic is a sore spot, and they are clearly uncomfortable with the conversation, don't be a savage and try to force them to talk about it. Table it for another time.

But do let them know that you want to discuss it at another time. Then, if they don't bring it up, you do it. Gently. Compassionately. Calculatedly.

Later, if you guys decide to keep dating, get counseling. A qualified counselor will help both of you identify potential problem areas and give you tools for how to work through them.

Atrocities

This harsh word is the only way to describe what some have experienced and it must be addressed and explored with your partner. It is vital to have open and honest discussions about any past experiences of abuse, whether it was emotional, mental, physical, or sexual in nature. If they've suffered this kind of trauma, it may be painful for your partner to recall and share their experiences, but it is essential to un-

DISCUSS EACH OTHER'S PASTS

derstand how these traumas have affected them. Some questions to consider:

- What was the exact nature of the abuse?
- When did the abuse occur?
- How long did it occur?
- How frequently did it occur?
- Who was the perpetrator? (Or were there multiple perpetrators?)
- How have they coped with the aftermath of such heinous acts?

It's also crucial to know if your partner was ever the abuser. If so, you need to understand the full context, their path of repentance, rehabilitation steps, and amends made.

Do not shy away from these tough questions or discussions. If you do, you will pay the price down the road. I don't care how much you're into them, don't let your attraction blind you to the impact of major issues like abuse. That's like ignoring a fire alarm because you're too wrapped up in a good book. Ignoring the alarm won't make the fire any less real or destructive. If there's a fire in your potential partner's past, you need to know about it now to avoid being burned later.

And speaking of fire...

That Old Flame Might Still Be Hot

Now it's time to move on to a topic that's a little less intense but no less important: past romantic relationships. This isn't just about sexual history (though we'll definitely get to that), but about all significant romantic connections, as each one can have a lasting effect. We all have a relationship resume, and each past partner is a reference, for better or worse.

The Ex Files: When The Past Is Still Present

Sometimes, exes aren't just a part of your partner's past, but the present too. Maybe they have children together and need to co-parent. Maybe they work together or share a friend group. *Maybe they still have feelings for them.*

In these situations, it's important to set clear boundaries and expectations. It's one thing for your partner to have a cordial relationship with their ex for the sake of their child. It's another thing entirely for them to be constantly texting, hanging out, or emotionally leaning on their ex.

Depending on the child's age, they should be in contact with their ex to some extent. To what extent is what you need to determine. (If they don't communicate with their child's other parent and their child is too young to communicate directly on their own, that's also a lead you need to chase down, because how do you have a whole child out here and not have some contact with them?)

If you're feeling uncomfortable with your partner's relationship with their ex, speak up. Don't accuse or attack, but do express your feelings and concerns. You might say something like, "I understand that you need to have a relationship with your ex for the sake of your kids, but I'm feeling uneasy about how much you text them. Can we discuss parameters?"

Approach this conversation as an ally, not an adversary. You're not trying to control your partner or erase their past but rather create a standard of trust for your future together.

If they have no child with their ex but they're still talking to them, ask them to explain the nature of their relationship. You have a right to know, not only for your peace of mind but also to gauge how fully committed they are to moving forward with you. Do you really want your future husband or wife to have casual conversations with their ex?

DISCUSS EACH OTHER'S PASTS

Exes And Oh-No's: Checking The Relationship Resume

When you're discussing past relationships with your partner, here are some key questions to consider:

- How many serious relationships have they had? And what do they consider "serious"?
- How long did each relationship last and why did they end?
- Do they still keep in touch with any of their exes? If so, how frequently?
- Are there financial ties, mutual friends, or unfinished business that keeps them connected to their ex?
- How do they feel about their ex(es) now?
- Did they split amicably or is their ongoing drama?
- Does the ex name-drop casually into your conversations way more often than you'd like?
- Have they ever cheated on someone before? If so, what were the circumstances?
- Is somebody from your partner's past gonna try to slash your tires or key your car when they find out about you?

The answers to these questions will tell you a lot about your partner, maybe more than they realize themselves. Recognize that this is an opportunity to examine their character, patterns of behavior, emotional stability, and more. Just be prepared for the possibility that some disclosures may change the course of your relationship. Don't let that be a deterrent, though.

To be clear, it's not the existence of your past that's the issue—it's whether you're shackled to it or you've grown from it.

Laying out your history can be downright terrifying. But you know what's even scarier? Waking up one day, years down the line, and as Tamia sang in her 2000 hit, "Stranger in My House," realizing you don't even know the person next to you. Or worse still, questioning if the real stranger is you.

Let's Talk About Sex, Baby

Okay, let's dive into the juicy stuff: sexual history. Most singles I know—and probably the ones you know too—are a long way from being virgins. If you happen to still be one by the way, know that there are millions of individuals that would pay money and give up virtually every material blessing they have to go back to that place of innocence.

God's best for you is to keep yourself sexually pure until marriage. In doing so, you avoid unhealthy soul ties, harmful comparisons, early pregnancy, disease, heartbreak, hurting God, and hurting others.

People who engage in premarital sex, whether by choice or through the traumatic experience of sexual assault, often face a complex aftermath. This can include emotional, physical, mental, and spiritual challenges stemming from those experiences.

If you've had the discipline to remain sexually pure, don't give it up. You'll be so glad on honeymoon night that you have no one to compare your spouse to. Regardless of what the sex feels like that night, it will be the best you've ever had. When you've had multiple sexual partners, sadly, that's not always true.

DISCUSS EACH OTHER'S PASTS

If you've had one or more sexual partners, it is what it is. You can't undo what's done. If you're a Christian, the blood of Jesus has washed your sins away and the Bible says you are new in Christ.

That said, though you've been forgiven, forgiveness doesn't erase your past, nor the consequences of your choices. As this new relationship you're considering gets serious, it's time to ask one of the scariest and hardest questions you'll ever have to ask this person you like: *What's your body count?*

Body Count: More Than Just A Number

It's important that you know who and what you're dealing with. If your future spouse has slept with someone you know, you probably want to hear it from them, not someone else.

If you're a man walking with your girl at the mall, and some random guy is like, "Yo, is that you, Keisha? Look at you!" Then to you he says, "Hey Bro, no disrespect, but me and Keisha go way back. She's a good girl. Best I ever had. Y'all be good now." And the way he looks at her while he walks away tells you a whole story about her past that she hasn't shared with you yet. Yeah, that's gonna be a problem.

Try to consider your future spouse the next time you think about sleeping with someone. Think about what it's going to feel like looking the one you love in the eye and telling them about all the people you gave yourself to.

You probably already know what it feels like to have someone ask you that question if you've ever been in a long-term relationship. I don't know anyone who feels good when they have to run down their "list."

So many people don't ask enough questions before they say, "I do." If I'm going to spend the rest of my life with someone, I don't want any surprises regarding past relationships. I want to know what I'm walking into so I can make an informed, intelligent choice about proposing to someone who slept with the entire high school football team or cheerleading squad.

I encourage you to have a tell-all conversation. Just sit down one day and let it fly. Begin by saying, "Tell me every single person you've slept with or had any sexual encounter with in your life." How much detail you want is up to you, but I would at least ask how many.

Here are a few other things to discuss when it comes to sexual history:

- **Sexual values and beliefs:** What is your partner's attitude towards sex? Do they see it as something sacred, reserved for marriage? Or something more casual? Do your beliefs align?

- **Sexual health:** Has your partner ever had an STD? Have they been tested recently? Do they have any sexual health concerns you should be aware of?

- **Sexual trauma:** Has your partner ever experienced sexual abuse, assault, or harassment? This can have a major impact on their sexual and emotional well-being.

- **Sexual experiences:** What kinds of sexual experiences has your partner had? Are there any that make you uncomfortable or that you need to discuss further?

- **Pornography and addiction:** Has your partner struggled with pornography or sexual addiction? This can create intimacy and trust issues in a relationship.

The purpose of these tough but necessary questions is to give you a crystal-clear perspective on who you're getting involved with because our sexual history shapes our present attitudes, behaviors, and even our physical and physiological responses to sex. Since sex is central to marriage, any lingering issues or trauma from past sexual experiences will likely resurface in the relationship at some point.

This conversation is not one to have on the first date, or even the second or third. Because the conversation is sexual in nature, you want to make sure you don't inadvertently give off the impression that you're having this talk because you're interested in having sex now. By the time you do talk about your sexual histories, you've clearly and mutually established a tone in your relationship that runs parallel with your values, which should include waiting till marriage to have sex.

SOUL TIES: THE SPIRITUAL AFTERMATH OF SEXUAL ENCOUNTERS

While we're on the topic of sexual history, I need y'all to lean in because we're about to tackle something that has been misunderstood, misquoted, and mystified in the Christian community: soul ties. Brace yourself because what I'm about to discuss is often left out of the church chat.

What Are Soul Ties?

First, let's be clear. You won't find the term 'soul tie' in your Bible, but the concept is implicitly present in the description of marriage as a union where two people become one flesh (Mark 10:8), and when Paul talks about sexual union creating a spiritual bond in 1 Corinthians 6:16. The idea is that when you sleep with someone, you're not just connecting with them physically, but you're also creating a deep spiritual and emotional bond - one that was intended to be reserved for the covenant of marriage.

Disrupting Divine Design

If we believe that God created sex exclusively for marriage and marriage for sex, they are intertwined by design. When we have sex outside of marriage then, we are disrupting and deviating from that design. We're engaging in a deeply intimate act without the commitment and covenant that's supposed to go with it, inviting complexity and confusion into what was designed to be a clear and straightforward path. We're taking something that was meant to be holy and making it common.

The Consequences Of Violating God's Design

There are rules, and when we have extramarital sex, we're asking God to change His rules to accommodate our choices. That's a theological conundrum because God's rules aren't up for negotiation. We can't ask Him to adjust His perfect design to fit our flawed decisions.

In essence, when you have sex with someone who's not your spouse, you're creating a bond with them that can have lasting spiritual and emotional consequences. You're tying your soul to theirs in a way that can be difficult to untangle, even after the physical relationship ends.

Some even say that in a very real sense, when you have sex with someone, you're marrying them in God's eyes, even if you've never said "I do" at the altar. That's why the real question isn't just "How many people have you slept with?" but "How many times have you been married?"

The Gender Divide: How Men And Women Experience Sex Differently

Now, I know this might ruffle some feathers, and many pastors and scholars might disagree. But to my knowledge, there's no biblical or scientific proof to disprove what I'm about to say next. In full transparency, however, let me state that this is my opinion, based on my experience conversing with and counseling men and women over the years.

I now believe that most men, generally speaking, are easily capable of having detached sex, while women struggle to understand how this is possible. I'm writing this from a male perspective, as a man who deeply loves his wife and is constantly trying to understand and please her.

What I've learned is this: the average man, whether it's your ex-boyfriend, your dad, or your son if he's grown, could walk into a room with seven women he's never seen before, never even look at their faces, have sex with each one of them in succession, thoroughly enjoy the physical pleasure of it, and then go grab a burger afterwards with absolutely no attachment whatsoever.

Ladies, I know this may be hard to digest, but please keep reading.

Instincts Vs. Integrity: The Inner Battle Of Every Man

Sociologists and anthropologists have studied this phenomenon extensively and often point to primal urges and the theory of evolutionary biology as an explanation. To put it simply, men are biologically wired for procreation with a variety of partners. It's the way our species survived for thousands of years.

Theoretically, it would take only thirty men to impregnate all the women in Cleveland, whereas a woman releases eggs only once a month, making her fertility much more limited. This is also why women, again, generally speaking, are more naturally inclined to seek out a stable, committed partner, as they bear the physical burden of pregnancy and childrearing.

Without getting too scientific here, if you look at the animal kingdom, you'll see similar patterns. The lion has his pride of lionesses, but most lionesses are only loyal to one lion. The buck has his herd of doe, but the doe only have their one buck. It's the same in the human world where men often desire multiple mates, while women are more prone to seeking a single mate.

But—and this is vital—we aren't animals. We are made in the image and likeness of God (Genesis 1:27). We have been given moral agency and the power of discernment and reasoning, something our friends in the animal kingdom don't possess to the degree we do, so none of these biological realities excuse sin.

Men absolutely have a duty to honor God and their spouses with their bodies and their minds, no matter how strong the temptation might be. But I do think it's important for women to understand how most men are wired so they have some insight into why some men behave the way they do.

The Origin Of These Differences: Fall Of Man Or God's Plan?

Now some might argue that these existential differences are the result of the fall of man. But if that's the case, why doesn't it seem to affect women in the same way? The argument could be made that this is how God designed men and women to be different, and that these differences existed even before sin entered the world.

Regardless of the origin of these differences, the reality remains. Men and women often experience sex and soul ties in fundamentally different ways. While this doesn't excuse infidelity or minimize the pain it causes, it does provide a lens for understanding.

Back To Eden: The Law Of First Mention And Sacred Union

But if we go back to the beginning, the law of first mention suggests that when God created Adam and Eve, Eve was enough for Adam as his companion, his partner, the one designed specifically for him. They were each other's person, the fulfillment of each other's needs—one man, one woman, one sacred union. This law of first mention sets a precedent that carries weight throughout the scriptures. There is no indication that a man would "cleave" to multiple wives. There is no mention of polygamy until after the fall.

Because we live in this fallen world, the reality is sin has distorted God's original model for sex and relationships. Polygamy was practiced by many of the men we revere in the Bible and it's still practiced in many cultures today. But just because something is common doesn't mean it's right or healthy.

Even still, the Bible, which admittedly has male bias, doesn't really depict women with multiple husbands. It's always the man with many wives, and the wives waiting on him. So there seems to be something innate, something biological, that allows men to compartmentalize sex in a way that women typically can't.

Now again, this does not justify men's behavior or mean that women are weaker in this sense. Far from it. I believe this emotional and spiritual depth possessed by women is a strength, a beautiful reflection of God's heart. But it can make women more vulnerable to soul ties.

Grounded By Love, Lured By Lust: A Tale Of Two Tendencies

In contrast to the way many men operate, women tend to approach sex and relationships with a different mindset. A woman can see an attractive man, and even if he's flirting with her and looks better than the man she's with, she'll be like, "Nah, I'm good. I love my man. He makes love to me, he takes care of me, he's the one I'm with." There's a loyalty and emotional connection there that most women can't or have no desire to turn off, even in the face of what would otherwise be temptation.

But a man? He can be just as in love with his woman, just as committed in his heart and soul, but still see another attractive woman and think, "Ooh, she fine." And if the opportunity presented itself to sleep with her and it wasn't wrong, he could do it and walk away without a second thought. He doesn't want to have children with her, he doesn't want to be in a relationship with her, he doesn't want to marry her. He just wants to sleep with her. In his mind, it's just physical release, completely separate from his emotional life.

A Word To Wives Dealing With Infidelity

If you're a woman whose husband has been unfaithful, understanding this difference in how men and women typically experience sex can be life-changing. And please know that his reason for cheating was not because you're inadequate or undesirable. It had nothing to do with your worth as a woman or wife. His actions are a reflection of his own weaknesses, failures, and brokenness.

For most men, sex is about physical gratification, not love or emotional connection. That other woman likely meant nothing to him beyond the moment. A man can be completely in love with his wife and still feel the urge to sleep with other women. This probably doesn't make you feel better, but it may provide some context and clarity, and may even help you process the pain.

A Plea To Single Women: Guard Your Garden

That's why I believe that for a woman, the act of sex, of being entered and receiving a man's seed and spirit into your body, is so much more intimate and impactful. It's not just about pleasure for a woman; it's about presence and that presence creates a deep attachment that can feel so much more intense than it does for a man.

This is also why I'm urging my single ladies to guard your hearts and your bodies. Don't let yourself be tied to a man who hasn't committed to you for life. Those soul ties are no joke and they can leave emotional scars that take a long time to heal.

A Message To Single Men: Stop Hoeing Around In These Gardens

As for my single brothers, I need you to grasp the weight of this. Understand that when you sleep with a woman, the sex will never be just physical. Whether you realize it or not, you're impacting her soul and possibly setting her up for years of emotional and spiritual debris that she'll have to clean up and clear out before she can fully devote herself to another. Do not sleep with any woman who is not your wife.

There's Also The Comparison Trap

In addition to the spiritual consequences, for men, the biggest issue is usually comparison. A man might find himself comparing his wife's body or sexual performance to that of a past partner, and that can definitely create problems in the marriage bed. So, single brothers, take heed. Don't fall into the trap of thinking that sex can ever be casual or without penalty, even if you're not contending with strong soul ties.

At the end of the day, our sexuality is a gift from God meant to be enjoyed within the covenant of marriage. Anything outside of that is a distortion of His design and carries very real spiritual and emotional consequences.

I know this is heavy stuff, but it's so important that we talk about it openly and honestly. We can't afford to ignore the spiritual implications of our sexual choices.

Culture And Conviction: The Pursuit Of Patience

In a culture that tells us to follow our desires wherever they lead, it takes courage and conviction to wait, to save ourselves for the one who will be our partner for life. It's not always easy, but it's always worth it. Because when you finally come together with your spouse, when you form that unbreakable bond under the blessing of God, you set yourself up for a lifetime of intimacy and fulfillment that is incomparable. The world could never.

Healing Grace: Breaking The Chains Of Past Choices

Here's the good news: No matter what your past looks like, no matter how many soul ties you may have formed, God's grace is bigger. He can heal every wound, break every chain, and restore every broken piece. His love for you is not contingent on your sexual purity or lack thereof.

If you're carrying the weight of past sexual sins or broken soul ties, bring them to the foot of the cross. Confess, repent, and receive the forgiveness and freedom that Christ bought for you with His blood. And then walk forward in the power of the Holy Spirit, committed to honoring God with your body and your heart.

WHEN THE PAST BECOMES A PROBLEM

As much as we want to believe love conquers all, sometimes a person's past is just too heavy to handle. When you're sizing up a potential life partner, you've got to do the math on their history. You're making an investment, so you've got to assess the risks and likely returns to determine if it's worth the price you'll have to pay. And I'm not just talking about money problems, although, let's keep it real, that's often a major factor. I'm also talking about the mental, emotional, and psychological toll that comes with the decisions we've made or the life we've lived. And y'all, this isn't about casting stones; it's about counting the cost of a shared future.

Their past decisions—be it their body count, the number of children they have, or the pile of debt they might be dragging—these are all factors that can weigh down a relationship. Look at every situation they've got going on and estimate the ongoing burdens that come with them. The drama queen or drama king that is their child's mother or father. The outstanding legal battles. The health issues and addictions. The obligations, entanglements, and limitations.

Healing Your Own Wounds

You may be trying to work through the pain of your own past. You're carrying your own baggage, your own scars, your own mistakes, and while you're doing the work to heal, it's a lot to carry someone else's load along with your own. When you come across someone whose history is an avalanche waiting to happen, it's okay to say, "With all that I have going on, I don't have the capacity to work through this with you. It's too much for me."

Again, I'm not saying that people can't change or that past mistakes define you forever. We serve a God of redemption and second chances. But I am saying that you need to be real about what someone is bringing into a relationship and what they're asking you to take on.

The Impact Of Your Decisions: Today's Choices, Tomorrow's Reality

Tomorrow, today will be in your past. That statement is deceptively simple. Let it sink in for a moment, and then consider this: your past (and present) decisions, whether you want them to or not, become your partner's future reality.

So, allow me to speak frankly here. Sometimes, a person might choose to leave you because they can't handle the weight of your past. They might look at you and say, *Wow, she's stunning. He's handsome. She's smart. He's kind. But the baggage... it's just too much.* They didn't wait their whole life to be dragged down by the mistakes someone else made. Be careful not to create a history too heavy for someone to willingly inherit. Handle your business now so that your past isn't a liability in your future.

The Past As Prologue

Your past is a part of you, but it doesn't have to define you. And your partner's past is a part of them, but it doesn't have to determine your future together. What matters is honesty, transparency, and a willingness to face the hard stuff head-on.

Ultimately, discussing the past is about creating a foundation for the future. It's about understanding where you've been so you can make intentional choices about where you're going. Don't run from these conversations, as uncomfortable as they might be. Embrace them as an opportunity to know each other more deeply, to build trust and intimacy, and to decide if this is a journey you want to take together.

Your past may be prologue, but your future is still unwritten. Keep moving forward, keep growing, and keep believing that your best days are ahead of you. And when you find someone who can handle your past and love you for your present, well, that's a beautiful thing indeed.

DISCUSS EACH OTHER'S PASTS

"Therefore, if anyone is in Christ, he is a new creation; old things have passed away; behold, all things have become new." - 2 Corinthians 5:17 (NKJV)

RULE 8
DISCUSS EACH OTHER'S PRESENT AND FUTURE EXPECTATIONS

"Love does not consist in gazing at each other, but in looking outward together in the same direction." - *Antoine de Saint-Exupéry*

FANTASIES VS. REALITIES: THE PRESENT AND THE FUTURE

Welcome to Rule 8—where we're taking a deep dive into the reality of your present life and where you envision going. When you're single and dating, it's easy to gloss over present issues and it's also fun to daydream and fantasize about what life might look like one day. But while you're floating on cloud nine, you better believe that reality is waiting for you back on the ground. Your present realities still exist and if Jesus doesn't come back first, tomorrow is on its way.

DISCUSS EACH OTHER'S PRESENT AND FUTURE EXPECTATIONS

In the previous chapters, we delved into the importance of self-awareness, knowing your non-negotiables, and never compromising on them. We discussed the significance of dating with purpose, having the Jesus talk, and understanding the dynamics of directional dating. Most recently, in Rule 7, we tackled discussing each other's pasts, and as necessary as it is to understand where your potential partner is coming from, it's equally important to know where they're headed because you're not just dating someone's past. You're dating their present and their future too.

As the wise Malcolm X once said, "The future belongs to those who prepare for it today." This sentiment rings especially true when it comes to dating and relationships. If you want a successful, fulfilling partnership that stands the test of time, you can't just wing it. You need to be proactive, intentional, and prepared because if you're not, you'll end up somewhere you never intended to be. When it comes to matters of the heart, that's a dangerous game to play.

In Rule 3, we talked about the importance of knowing your non-negotiables. These are the dealbreakers, the must-haves, the no-way-no-hows that you absolutely cannot compromise on in a relationship. And while it's crucial to have these standards clear in your own mind, it's just as important to communicate them clearly to your partner because your non-negotiables don't just exist in a vacuum. They're directly tied to your current circumstances and your future goals. And that's where discussing your present and future expectations comes in.

If your non-negotiables are the blueprint, your present situation is the ground on which you're building, and your future expectations are the structure you're trying to create. If these three elements aren't aligned, you're setting yourself up for a shaky, unstable relationship that's bound to crumble under pressure.

Talking about the future, especially early on in a relationship, can feel presumptuous or even premature. But if you're truly dating with intention, if you're really seeking a godly partnership, then these conversations are essential. Because you're not just dating for fun or for the moment. You're dating for the possibility of forever. And forever is a long time to be stuck with someone who doesn't share your vision or your values.

Assume The Position

As Christians, preparing for the future isn't just about anticipating, it's about positioning. By honoring God with our choices, living purposefully according to practical principles, and exercising integrity and transparency in discussing our expectations, we place ourselves in a position to win with God's favor, creating space for Him to bless us in our relationships. While our plans may change, His plans prevail (Psalm 33:11), and we can trust that we're moving toward the kind of relationship that honors Him and nourishes us. That said, here are some key areas you need to discuss with your partner.

Emotional Health: The Backbone Of Dating And Marriage

As Peter Scazzero says, "It's impossible to be spiritually mature while remaining emotionally immature." It's also impossible to have a healthy marriage if one or both partners are emotionally unhealthy. We all have areas that we need to improve in. Even if it's not trauma-based, just the general wear and tear of life can leave us drained and in need of rejuvenation.

Dealing with past hurts and traumas is a significant aspect of improving our emotional health. But beyond that, it's about developing the resilience and fortitude to withstand the inevitable ups and downs of life and love. It's about being able to communicate your needs and emotions in a healthy way, without resorting to manipulation, passive-

DISCUSS EACH OTHER'S PRESENT AND FUTURE EXPECTATIONS

aggression, or stonewalling. It's something we work on every single day, through our choices, our habits, and our relationship interactions.

Emotional health is the backbone of dating and marriage because, let's face it: relationships are emotional. They bring up all kinds of feelings, from joy and excitement to fear and frustration. If you're not equipped to handle those emotions in a constructive way, things can go south, really fast.

Emotional Readiness Checkpoint

So, how do you know if you're emotionally ready for a committed relationship? Start by asking yourself some tough questions:

- Have you dealt with your past hurts and hang-ups?

- Are you able to talk about your past without getting defensive or shutting down?

- Are you able to communicate your feelings in a healthy way, or do you tend to stuff them down or lash out in anger? Can you express your needs and desires clearly and respectfully?

- Do you have a strong sense of self, or do you tend to lose yourself in relationships? Are you able to maintain your own identity and boundaries even when you're deeply connected to someone else?

- Do you take responsibility for your actions and emotions, or do you tend to blame others when things go wrong? Can you apologize and make amends when necessary?

If you're not sure about the answers to these questions, that's okay. Emotional health is a journey too. But it's important to be honest with yourself about where you are on that journey, and what work you still need to do.

The same goes for your partner. Watch how they handle stress and conflict. Notice how they communicate their feelings and needs. Pay attention to how they treat others, not just you.

If your partner is unwilling to be transparent about their mental health, or if they consistently resort to unhealthy coping mechanisms like withdrawal or emotional manipulation, be cautious. As we've discussed throughout this book, you deserve someone who is committed to their own growth and well-being, and who is willing to do the hard work of building an emotionally healthy relationship.

But even if you and your partner are relatively emotionally healthy, there will still be challenges along the way. Conflict is inevitable in any relationship; it's how you handle that conflict that matters most.

That's where emotional intelligence comes in. Emotional intelligence is the ability to recognize and manage your own emotions, as well identify or empathize with the emotions of others. It's being able to communicate effectively, especially when you're having "heated fellowship." Can you empathize with your partner's perspective, even when you disagree?

Cultivating Emotional Intelligence: Tips For Effective Communication

Developing emotional intelligence takes time and practice. You need a big heart, the ability to keep your head, and the skill of knowing how to read the room, that is, your partner's demeanor and reactions. When you have high emotional intelligence, you can take on the tough stuff in your relationships without losing your cool or your connection.

So, how can you cultivate emotional intelligence in your relationship? Here are a few tips:

DISCUSS EACH OTHER'S PRESENT AND FUTURE EXPECTATIONS

- **Practice active listening.** When your partner is laying their heart out, lock in. Give them your full attention. Put down your phone, make eye contact, and really listen to what they're saying. Reflect back what you've heard to make sure you've understood them correctly.

- **Use "I" statements.** When expressing your own feelings or needs, use "I" statements instead of "you" statements. For example, instead of saying, "You always make me feel neglected," try saying, "I feel neglected when we don't spend quality time together." This way, nobody's playing the blame game.

- **Take responsibility for your own emotions.** Remember, your feelings are valid, but they are not your partner's responsibility. It's up to you to manage your emotions and to communicate them respectfully. Own your feelings, don't let them own you.

- **Practice forgiveness.** Holding onto grudges or resentment will only poison your relationship in the long run. When your partner makes a mistake or hurts your feelings, try to give them the benefit of the doubt. Be willing to forgive (regardless) and move forward, as long as your partner taken responsibility for their actions and make amends.

Emotional health and emotional intelligence are not optional in a healthy relationship. The good thing is, they are skills that can be learned and developed over time.

A relationship is only as strong as the emotional foundation it's built on. When that foundation is solid,

there's no limit to the love, joy, and intimacy you can create together.

Character: The Substance Behind The Behavior

Now, let's get into character. We all want to make a good impression when we're getting to know someone. We want to highlight our best qualities and maybe gloss over some of our less-than-stellar traits, but the truth always comes out eventually. When it does, you want to make sure you're with someone whose character you can count on.

So, what exactly do I mean by character? Well, it's a combination of a person's moral qualities, their integrity, their work ethic, their values, and their behavior patterns. It's who they are when no one is watching. It's how they treat people who can't do anything for them. It's what they stand for and what they won't stand for.

Character matters because it's the substance behind a person's behavior; what comes to light when the masks fall away and the social scripts end. You're not just partnering with someone's good looks or their charming personality. You're partnering with their whole self, flaws and all. If their character is lacking, it's only a matter of time before that starts to cause some serious problems.

So, take a long hard look at your partner's character. Do they keep their word? Do they show up on time and follow through on their commitments? Do they treat service workers with respect and kindness? Do they gossip or speak negatively about others behind their back?

These may seem like small things, but they're actually very telling. Someone who cuts corners or treats others poorly in their everyday life is likely to do the same in their relationship. And that's not something you want to sign up for.

DISCUSS EACH OTHER'S PRESENT AND FUTURE EXPECTATIONS

When Money Talks, You Should Listen

Money talks, and in relationships, it can either promise security or threaten stability, which is why it's critical to lay your financial cards on the table before they become a house of cards.

Think about it. If your partner has a history of not paying their bills on time, of racking up debt, of living beyond their means... what does that say about their character? About their ability to commit? About their willingness to sacrifice for the greater good of your relationship?

When you're building a life with someone, you're not just merging your hearts and dreams. You're also merging your finances. If one of you has a ton of debt or a terrible credit score, that can put a serious strain on your relationship. Now, I'm not saying that a low credit score is an automatic dealbreaker. We all make mistakes and sometimes life just happens. But it is something you need to discuss.

Issues related to money are one of the foremost causes for divorce in the country. Most people decide to get married without a concrete financial plan. For one reason or another, they neglect to talk about the interpersonal dynamics related to money; consequently, they leave their financial situation, and their relationship, to chance. Couples think that if they avoid talking about money and they love each other enough, their finances will work out effortlessly and effectively, as if their money has a will of its own.

Newsflash: Finances do not just work out; they have to be worked out.

Let's Talk Money, Honey!

Without a solid plan for how you will handle money, financial troubles will likely arise. In fact, these troubles tend to increase when not handled aggressively and appropriately. You can save yourselves years of pain and stress by engaging in candid conversations regarding your views, beliefs, thoughts, and plans concerning this important subject.

Given the artificial nature of relationships in the very beginning—when you're still trying to impress them and they're still not being completely real with you about some embarrassing habit they have—money is probably not a good first date subject. However, if you've been dating awhile and the relationship is serious and moving in the direction of covenant commitment, have the money talk.

Money is as important an issue as any to discuss before marriage. If you and the person you're dating have completely divergent views about money and its significance in your lives, it will inevitably lead to strife.

Her Desire vs. His Dollars

As a woman, ask yourself how much money you feel you need to be happy. If you come from a home where your father took care of all your mother's financial needs, then that may be what you expect and long for. If you were raised in an environment where your dad was absent, leaving your mother with sole financial responsibility, then your views may be different.

Maybe you expect or are determined to earn a living alongside your spouse. Perhaps you are enjoying the rewards of a fulfilling career or profitable business and want to continue to work to help your husband build a solid, financial future for the betterment of your family. Maybe you have a higher earning potential. The important thing is to be honest regarding your true thoughts, opinions, and emotions and listen carefully to the way your potential spouse feels.

His Ego vs. Her Income

As a man, ask yourself if you are okay with your wife earning more money than you. Because like it or not, my brother, in many instances, she just might. Are you intimidated by a woman who out-earns you? The truth is, she may not need you for your money; she needs you for your ministry. Can you handle that?

Marry Reality, Not Potential: A Hard Look At Your Partner's Finances

One of the most important statements I can make to you as a single person is this: Don't just marry potential, marry reality! I know it's tempting to look at that fine man or woman and see all the amazing things they could be. You see their kindness, their intelligence, their sexy smile, and you think, "With a little love and support, they could conquer the world!" And hey, there's nothing wrong with seeing the best in someone and encouraging them to reach their full potential.

But potential doesn't pay the bills. Potential doesn't put food on the table or keep the lights on. And potential sure as heck doesn't guarantee a stable, secure future together. That's why you need to take a good look at your partner's financial reality before you even think about putting a ring on it or accepting a ring. You need a close-up view of their entire financial picture.

Show Me The Money: A Deep Dive Into Your Partner's Pockets

So, how do you get that information? It's simple: you ask for it. You need to sit down with your partner and have a frank, open conversation about money. Lay it all out on the table, no matter how uncomfortable it might feel, because what is not revealed now will come back to bite you later. If your partner has a history of financial irresponsibility or instability, ignoring it won't make it go away. In fact, it'll probably only get worse once you're married and your finances are linked.

When engaging in conversations about money, one of the first points to discuss is how much money each of you have presently. The answers that you both provide should not include your financial vision statements, or how much money you plan to have in the future. This should be a straightforward response indicating your present worth. You each need to know what the other's money looks like right now.

To see money matters for what they truly are, show each other current bank statements, and any other statements revealing financial status. Bank statements not only prove how much money you currently have, they demonstrate spending habits. Our spending habits show what we value—and what we don't.

Is Love Blind Or Just Broke?

Ladies, if your man is drowning in debt and can barely hold down a job, you need to think about whether that's the reality you want. I don't care how handsome he is or how much he makes you laugh. At the end of the day, looks and humor won't keep a roof over your head or food in your belly.

And brothers, if that woman you're falling for expects you to take care of her financially like her daddy did, you need to ask yourself if that's a dynamic you're willing to accept. It doesn't matter how beautiful she is or how much she strokes your ego. If you need her income to maintain the household you plan on sharing, she needs to know that.

You must base your decisions about the future on who and where your partner is right now, not who you hope they'll become. Marriage is a lifetime commitment and you want to be sure that you're committing to a partner who is financially stable, responsible, and on the same page as you when it comes to money.

DISCUSS EACH OTHER'S PRESENT AND FUTURE EXPECTATIONS

Key Financial Discussion Points

So, what should you be looking for? Here are a few things to discuss and consider:

- **Income**: How much money does your partner currently make? Is it enough to support the lifestyle you want? Are you comfortable being the sole breadwinner or do you expect your partner to contribute financially?

- **Debt**: Does your partner have any outstanding debts like student loans, credit card balances, or car payments? How much do they owe and what's their plan for paying it off?

- **Savings**: Does your partner have any money saved for emergencies or long-term goals? How much do they have in their checking and savings accounts?

- **Investments**: Has your partner made any investments like a 401k or IRA? How much are they contributing, and what are their long-term financial goals?

- **Insurance**: Does your partner have life insurance or other important policies in place? How much coverage do they have, and who are the beneficiaries?

- **Spending habits**: Does your partner live within their means, or do they have a tendency to overspend? Are they impulsive with money or do they carefully budget and plan their purchases?

As with other topics we've discussed, conversations about money are not one-time conversations. Your financial situation will change over time—you might get a raise, lose a job, have a financial emergency... the list goes on. The key is to keep the lines of communication open, to revisit your plans and adjust as needed. These might not be the most romantic topics to discuss on a date, but it is what it is. You don't want to find yourself in a situation where financial stress and disagreements are tearing your relationship apart.

But there's more to it than avoiding potential problems. It's also about creating a bright, solid future as a team. When you agree on money, you're investing in a mutual fund of trust, goals, and dreams that will yield dividends in all aspects of your life together. You can make smart decisions about spending and saving, and you can support each other's goals and dreams. You can save for a down payment on a house, start a business, travel the world, or whatever else your hearts desire.

And that's what God wants for you. He wants you to thrive and prosper in every area of your life, even as your soul prospers (3 John 1:2), including your finances. But He also expects you to be wise and responsible with the resources He's given you.

If you or your partner are hesitant to talk about finances, this too might be a reason to slow down. Because if you can't talk openly and honestly about money, how can you expect to talk about all the other challenges that come with building a life together?

CAREER AND CAREER DEMANDS: THE SILENT RELATIONSHIP KILLER

Let's talk about another big topic that can have a huge impact on your relationship: careers. Now, I know some of you might be thinking, "What does my job have to do with my love life?" Everything, especially as it relates to your future.

You probably know what your partner does, where they work, and maybe you've heard a thing or two about their coworkers. But do you really understand how their career affects them on a day-to-day basis? Do you know how many hours they're pulling each week, whether they're expected to be on call 24/7, or if they're racking up frequent flyer miles faster than you can say "business trip"?

The Devil's In The (Career) Details

These details might seem small but they add up and they matter. And if you're not paying attention, they can sneak up on your relationship and create an environment that is ripe for disappointment and dissension due to unmet or unspoken expectations.

Take, for example, a partner who's working around the clock, always tethered to their devices, and unable to be fully present when you're together. That kind of schedule leaves little room for precious quality time, intimate conversations, or even a decent night's sleep. Over time, that disconnect can breed hostility, loneliness, and a feeling that your relationship is playing second fiddle to their career.

Or maybe your partner's job involves a lot of travel, whisking them away to far-flung cities for days or weeks at a time. The reality of long-distance love is seldom as rosy as it appears in rom coms. The missing, the longing, the sheer logistics of trying to maintain a connection across time zones and area codes - it's tough.

It's not just about the schedule or the travel, though. It's also about the emotional weight your partner carries home from work each day. Maybe they're shouldering the stress of a high-stakes project, the pressure of an overbearing boss, or the constant jockeying and politics of a competitive workplace.

Their occupational stress doesn't just vanish once they're off—it walks right through the front door with them. It seeps into their mood, their energy, their very presence in the relationship. They might be more irritable or short-tempered, less engaged, or just too exhausted to give you the attention and affection you need.

But wait, there's more! You also have to talk about where they are career-wise. Are they looking to stay put, move up, or switch things up completely? Is your partner's career a stable source of income or are they job hopping? Are they ruthlessly ambitious, forever chasing that next promotion, that next big client, that next brass ring? These talks help you both know what to expect and set the tone for how you can support each other's vocational aspirations.

We've already covered how money woes can be a major source of tension in a relationship. Well, if one partner is always stressing about making ends meet while the other is blissfully oblivious, that's a recipe for resentment.

So, what's a love-struck single to do? Thankfully, none of this is too big to handle. It all comes down to talking it out and being willing to figure things out together. You've got to approach your career challenges as a team, not as two separate entities competing for attention and resources. It means having a shared vision for your future, putting in the work to make it a reality, and being willing to make adjustments as needed, even when the demands of the daily grind are pulling you in different directions.

It could also mean having a come-to-Jesus moment about whether your careers are truly compatible with the kind of relationship you want to build. If one of you is married to your job and the other is yearning for a more balanced life, that's a fundamental disconnect that no amount of date nights or "I love you's" can fix.

Your careers should be a source of fulfillment and purpose, not a source of constant stress and strain on your relationship. If you're not willing to do what it takes to find that sweet spot, then you're not setting yourselves up for long-term success as a couple. Don't shy away from candid conversations about your work lives. In the end, your relationship is the most important job you'll ever have.

DISCUSS EACH OTHER'S PRESENT AND FUTURE EXPECTATIONS

Kids: The Great Family Planning Debate

Whether you already have kids or you're thinking about having them in the future, this is a fundamental issue that you need to be on the same page about from the very beginning. You may have already covered it in your non-negotiables, but there's nothing wrong with making sure. If one of you has always dreamed of being a parent and the other is adamant about being child-free, that's a major incompatibility that will be difficult to overcome.

Let's say you both want kids. Great! How many kids do you want? How soon after marriage would you want to start trying? Are you open to adoption or fertility treatments if needed? These are all important questions to discuss and agree on before you take the plunge into marriage and parenthood.

If you already have kids from a previous relationship, there's a whole other set of questions to consider. Are you ready to be a bonus parent? How will you blend your families? Is your partner willing to take on that role? How will you handle discipline and parenting decisions? Will you have a united front or will you defer to the biological parent? If you're the one with a child, can your partner discipline your son or daughter once you get married? How will you co-parent with your exes?

Parenting is a team sport and you need to make sure you're both playing by the same rules.

But it's not just about the big picture stuff, it's also about the daily realities of raising kids. What kind of parenting style do you envision? Will you be strict or lenient? Will you prioritize structure or creativity? Are you going to be the helicopter parent or the free-range parent?

And what about faith? How do you plan on passing down your spiritual beliefs? Will church attendance be a non-negotiable or will you leave it up to your kids to decide when they're older? What about faith-based rituals like praying before meals, bedtime prayers, and biblical teachings in everyday life? Talk about these things. Pray about these things.

And let's not forget about the financial implications of raising a family. Kids are expensive, y'all. From diapers and daycare to college tuition and beyond, the costs can add up fast. Are you both on the same page about how you'll handle these expenses? Do either of you pay or receive child support? If so, how will this affect your budget? What if your partner is behind on child support? You do know that when it's time to file taxes, under certain circumstances, the government can garnish the refund check you would've otherwise received if your partner owes backpay, don't you? If you don't want to find yourself unexpectedly in this situation, make sure you know the real deal on everything.

These are just a few of the hundreds of questions you'll need to navigate when it comes to parenting because once you're in it, your life will never be the same. And if you're not on the same page about your parenting values and goals, it can lead to a lot of conflict down the road.

Even if you do agree on all the big stuff, know that parenting is still going to be a wild ride. You're going to have moments of pure joy and love, and you're also going to have moments of frustration and exhaustion. You're going to disagree about screen time and bedtime and whether or not to let your kid eat that questionable piece of food off the floor. With older kids, you'll have to figure out curfews, dating, and the never-ending battle over chores.

You may find yourself in a situation where your bonus child lashes out and says, "You can't tell me what to do because you're not my

DISCUSS EACH OTHER'S PRESENT AND FUTURE EXPECTATIONS

mother [or father]!" Then what do you do? How will you and your spouse address these situations?

In those moments, you might question if you're in over your head, but if you're committed to each other, you'll find a way to make it work. You'll find your unique rhythm as a family, that perfect blend of chaos and harmony, if you're willing to communicate openly.

Living Arrangements: Home Is Where The Heart (And The Housework) Is

It's time to roll up our sleeves and dig into the down and dirty of domestic life. That's right, we're talking about household duties - the unsung heroes of every happy home.

When you're building a nest together, you're going to have to be intentional about the day-in, day-out dynamics of living together, and that means figuring out who's doing what around the house. How you work it out is up to you, but do work it out.

Deciding who does what around the house is more than just maintaining a clean and organized living space. It's a tangible expression of the respect and care you have for each other and your shared environment. If one person feels burdened with all or the majority of the household chores, it could turn into emotional fatigue and that fatigue will translate to other issues.

Chore Wars: Divide And Conquer

A word of caution here: Don't assume that traditional gender roles will dictate who does what. To make sure you're both pulling your weight, sit down and have an honest conversation about it. Maybe you're a master chef and your partner is a laundry wizard. Great! Divide and conquer. Or maybe you both hate cleaning bathrooms with a passion.

In that case, consider investing in a cleaning service or taking turns tackling the dreaded task.

The point is, you've got to find a system that works and feels fair to both of you. Be willing to adjust as needed because work schedules change. Kids come along. Health issues arise. The goal is not to have a perfect 50/50 split of every single task. The goal is to have a partnership, where both of you are contributing to the smooth running of your household in a way that works for your unique situation.

Location, Location, Location

Your living situation is also a reflection of your shared values and goals. Are you both on the same page about your long-term housing plans? Do you need a lot of personal space or do you thrive on togetherness? Do you want to buy a house together someday, or are you happy renting for the foreseeable future? Do you envision yourself living in the city, the suburbs, or somewhere more rural? If one of you dreams of a white picket fence and a big backyard, and the other can't imagine leaving the hustle and bustle of your city's metropolitan area, that's a pretty big disconnect.

Ultimately, a home is not defined by its location, square footage, or amenities. After all, it's the people within a space that bring life to it, that make it feel safe and peaceful. So, whether it's urban energy or serene suburbia that calls to you, make sure it's a mutual call. Because the true essence of home is where your lives, not just your living spaces, intertwine.

PREPARING FOR THE GOLDEN YEARS AND PROTECTING YOUR ASSETS

For some of you, retirement might feel like a lifetime away. But trust me, it sneaks up on you faster than you think.

DISCUSS EACH OTHER'S PRESENT AND FUTURE EXPECTATIONS

So, start the conversation now. What do you want your retirement to look like? Do you want to travel the world? Volunteer? Start a second career? Spoil your grandkids rotten? And more importantly, how will you get there? What kind of savings do you need to have? What kind of investments should you be making? What kind of lifestyle changes might you need to make now to ensure a comfortable retirement later?

The answers to these questions require research and forethought, and there are no one-size-fits-all answers. The earlier you start planning though, the more options you'll have down the road.

Prenups: Hope For The Best, Plan For The Worst

If you're really serious about building a life together, you might want to consider a prenup. I know, I know. It's not the most romantic thing in the world but hear me out. A prenup isn't about planning for divorce. It's about protecting both of you and your assets in case the worst happens. It's a way to have an honest conversation about your financial expectations and to create a plan that feels fair and equitable to both of you.

A prenup, short for prenuptial agreement, is a legal contract that outlines how assets will be divided in the event of a divorce. It's not about planning for failure—it's about protecting yourselves and your loved ones, just in case.

You may be in love now, but love is a choice, an action, a commitment; it's not a guarantee. While I hope and pray that your marriage lasts a lifetime, I also know that sometimes, despite our best efforts, things don't work out the way we planned. So, have the conversation. Look at your assets, your debts, your family situation. Consider what you want to protect and provide for, in good times and in bad.

Most of all, approach it with love and understanding. A prenup doesn't reveal a lack of trust or a lack of love. It's reveals your wisdom and commitment to steward the blessings God has given you. It's about recognizing that marriage is not just a spiritual union, but a legal and financial one as well. It's about entering into marriage with eyes wide open, with a shared understanding of what you're both bringing to the table and what you're taking from it if things don't work out.

The Fair Approach To Prenups

I want to take a moment to address a specific situation that many couples find themselves in—when one partner comes into the marriage with significantly more assets than the other. In this scenario, it's all too easy for the partner with fewer assets to feel insecure or even guilty about the imbalance. They might worry that their love will be questioned, that their motives will be suspect, or that they'll be seen as a "gold digger" just looking for a payday.

If you're the partner with less financial means, you have a unique opportunity to show your partner that your love is pure, that your commitment is real, that you're not trying to lay claim to what isn't yours.

How do you do this? By being the one to bring up the prenup.

If you're stepping into a marriage and your pockets are light while your partner's are fat, it's on you to broach the subject of a prenup. That's right, by proactively suggesting a prenup, you're not just protecting your partner's assets - you're protecting your relationship. You're saying, "I love you for you, not for what you have. I'm not here to take anything from you. And I want you to know that no matter what happens, I'm not in this for the money. If we don't make it, all I want is my fair share of what I helped us build."

It's a bold move, to be sure. It takes courage, vulnerability, and a sense of integrity. But when you approach the conversation with an open heart and a clear conscience, you're sending a very clear signal to your partner, removing any doubt about your intentions. This can actually bring you closer together as a couple. It can deepen your bond, strengthen your trust, and give you a sense of peace and security as you move toward marriage.

Conversations That Count: The Path To True Intimacy

We've covered a lot of ground here. From the emotional to the practical, from the romantic to the mundane... it's a lot to take in. If you're not willing to have these conversations, you're not ready for that "till death do us part" type of life. It's in the day-to-day decisions and conversations, the lighthearted banter and the serious strategizing, where true partnership is forged.

So, don't be afraid to have the tough talks. Don't be afraid to get real and raw and vulnerable with each other. When you bring that kind of purpose to your relationship, when you face the challenges of making a life together, that's when you establish a love that will stand both the test of time and the trials of life.

RULE 9
HURRY UP AND TAKE YOUR TIME

"Fools rush in, but the wise take their time."

Caught In Cupid's Current

Falling in love is a feeling like no other. It's the kind of feeling that consumes you, body and soul. It's second only to that life-changing moment when you truly encounter Christ and are filled with His Spirit. When you're in the throes of new love, it's a sensation that defies description, one that only those currently swept up in it can fully understand. Now, don't get me wrong, those of us who have found a lasting, proven, Christ-centered love wouldn't trade it for the world. But that doesn't negate the sheer intensity of those early days—the sleepless nights, the marathon phone calls, the way every love song seems to be speaking directly to your heart.

When you fall in love, you fall hard and fast. It's not a slow, gentle slide—it's a full-on free fall. One moment you're going about your life, the next you're head over heels, plummeting into a whirlwind of emotions. Your heart races when you're near them, and you find yourself caught between exhilaration and anxiety, nerves and giddiness. It's a feeling so good, so all-encompassing, that it's hard to imagine anything could possibly go wrong.

Love's Illusion Confusion

If this description hits a little too close to home, if you're nodding along and thinking, "That's exactly how I feel," then I've got two words for you: SLOW DOWN. Trust me, I know how incredible it is, how everything in you wants to dive headfirst into this new love. But my years of counseling couples on the brink of disaster have taught me one thing—things are not always as they seem. People have a way of putting their best foot forward when they're trying to win someone over, only to reveal their true colors once that ring is securely on theirs or their partner's finger.

Conniving Casanovas

I've seen it happen too many times to count. Smooth-talking brothers who waltz into the church, sweep one of my precious spiritual daughters off her feet, and convince her to marry him, only to show her who he really is the moment the vows are exchanged. Suddenly, he stops coming to church, starts turning her against me and the ministry, isolating her from the sound biblical teaching that would give her the wisdom to see through his manipulation.

Deceptive Divas

But it's not just the brothers who can be deceiving. I've watched women ensnare the hearts of the good sons in our church, only to turn around and withhold the love, support, and encouragement that every husband needs to thrive. It breaks my heart to see singles who were on fire for the Lord, making strides in their finances, education, and future, throw it all away by hitching their wagon to the wrong person. If you're picking up on a note of passionate pessimism here, it's only because I've seen the devastation of a bad marriage one too many times and I don't want you to become another statistic.

Love On The Brain: When Emotions Short-Circuit Logic

So, let me reiterate my advice: no matter how incredible everything feels in this moment, no matter how your heart swells with warmth and excitement, you need to pump the brakes and take things slow. When you're madly in love, it's like your brain gets hijacked. You're desperately trying to juggle the demands of daily life with the all-consuming emotions coursing through your veins, but it's a losing battle. Suddenly, everything else takes a backseat—even your relationship with God.

God's Compassion In The Chaos Of Love

Here's the beautiful truth: God understands. He doesn't condemn you for being swept up in these feelings. After all, He's the mastermind behind both the selfless, spiritual love that flows from the Holy Spirit and the passionate, romantic love that ignites between a man and a woman. He wired us for both.

Don't beat yourself up if your devotion to prayer has been overshadowed by daydreams of your new love. Don't feel guilty if you've been a little less present with your friends and family lately. The point here is not to rob yourself of what will hopefully be your last experience with dating and falling for someone new. Just keep a clear head, slow down, and make sure you're not rushing into something you'll regret.

Single Parents: It's Not Just About You Anymore

To all the single parents, you too, should give yourself some grace if you haven't been the most attentive mom or dad recently. It's completely understandable. You're not a bad daughter, a terrible friend, or a neglectful father. You're simply in love.

While we're on the subject of single parents, I want to make something clear. The moment you had a child, your dating life stopped being just about you. Every decision you make, every person you bring into your life, affects not only you, but your little ones as well. I don't care how amazing this new person seems, how swept off your feet you are—your family's well-being has to come first. It's time to take a step back, catch your breath, and really look at how your children are handling this new person in their lives.

Are they ready for the seismic shift from a single-parent household to a blended family? Is your new love bringing their own children into the mix? Have you prepared your kids for the potential upheaval this could cause in their lives? I know what you're thinking—how could someone so wonderful possibly cause any grief for your children? Well, any change, even a positive one, can be a source of grief for a child. And there's no bigger change than suddenly having to share their mother or father with someone they're not sure they can trust yet. So, if you've been floating on cloud nine for the past year, it's time to plant your feet back on the ground and make sure everyone is adjusting to this new reality.

Time Out

My advice to all singles at this point in the relationship is to back up off each other for a minute. You know that old saying, "Can't see the forest for the trees"? That's exactly what's happening when you're consumed by the intensity of new love. When you're smack dab in the middle of it, it's impossible to see the bigger picture. That's why sometimes you need to create some distance to gain clarity.

It's time to pause and get some perspective. As exciting as the emotional rush can be, you need clear eyes to evaluate if this relationship is heading in a godly direction.

I like to think of it as pressing the "slow-motion replay" button, like during a big football game. When a controversial play happens, the officials review it in super slo-mo to make the right call. They focus on details that were overlooked in real-time. Relationship red flags can slip by in the heat of the moment just like that unnoticed foul in the game. Press your slow-motion replay button, review the game tape, and check for any penalties you may have missed.

Love On Lockdown:
Why Boundaries Are Your Best Friend

I know it's not easy to hit pause when your heart is racing a mile a minute, but a brief timeout now will save you a lifetime of heartache later. As counterintuitive as it may seem, there is such a thing as spending too much time together. When you're in each other's faces constantly, it's all too easy to make one of the biggest mistakes of your life—jumping into bed before you're married.

Sex makes everything more complicated and can blind you to the real issues in your relationship. I know you think you're strong enough to resist temptation, but when you're in this deep and you're with the one you love, it's like trying to hold back the ocean with a broom. It's not happening, friend. Not unless you put real boundaries in place.

So, it's time to put away the rose-colored glasses and get real about who this person is and whether you're truly ready for the life-altering commitment of marriage. This isn't just about mind-blowing sex and splitting the rent. This is your future we're talking about. You need to be absolutely certain that this is the person you want to wake up next to every day for the rest of your life.

The Wisdom Of Slowing Down

That's why I'm telling you today: hurry up and take your time. I know it sounds counterintuitive, but trust me, it's essential. When you're in love, it's crucial that you give yourself the space to think clearly, to evaluate your relationship objectively, and to make sure that you're not rushing into something you're not ready for.

Now, I'm not saying that you should put your relationship on hold indefinitely. There's a difference between godly caution and unnecessary delay. What I am saying is that you need to be intentional about your pace. You need to make sure that you're moving forward in a way that honors God and respects the seriousness of the commitment you're considering.

By taking a step back, you give yourself the opportunity to regain your perspective. You can reconnect with the people and things that matter most to you, and you can take an honest look at your relationship from a distance. You might realize that there are issues you need to address, or you might find that your feelings are even stronger than you thought.

You're not playing games or testing your partner's loyalty, you're creating space for reflection, prayer, and discernment. It's about making sure that you're moving forward in a way that aligns with God's will for your life.

So, here's my advice—sit down with your partner and agree to set some boundaries around your time together in this season. Establish specific days and times for seeing each other and even for phone calls. And when you do talk, skip the lovey-dovey fluff and get down to business. It's time to dig into the nitty-gritty of where this relationship is headed.

For starters, if you're not attending the same church, you need to have a serious discussion about where you'll be worshipping together. Who's going to have to say goodbye to their pastor and church family? Is this going to be an issue? What about any baggage from past relationships or family drama? How are you planning to tackle those challenges as a couple? And let's not forget about money—remember Rule 8? It's time to lay all your cards on the table and figure out how you're going to handle any debt or credit issues as a team. Basically, you need to cover all your bases and discuss anything and everything that comes with building a life together.

The idea of spending less time together might feel like torture but take comfort in knowing this isn't a break-up. You're not mad at each other. You're not seeing other people. You're simply making a mature, responsible choice to do what's best for your God-centered relationship and your potential future as husband and wife. You're not settling for average here—you're committed to praying, thinking, and making wise decisions before diving in headfirst.

Don't be shocked if, once you have some space to breathe and think, you start noticing some things about your partner that you're not so crazy about. That's not a bad thing—that's just reality. Nobody's perfect, including you and this person you're falling for. The more you can uncover before you say "I do," the better. And believe me, once you're married, you'll discover even more surprises along the way.

A Call To Check Your Motivations

Now is a good time to get real with yourself about why you want to get married in the first place. Yeah, I know—you're convinced they're the one, that you've "never felt this way before," that it "doesn't get any better than this." But do you truly understand your motivations for wanting to tie the knot? Are you just afraid of being alone? Feeling the pressure of your biological clock? Trying to fill the void left by a past heartbreak?

Maybe you're caught up in a cycle of sexual sin and you think marriage will magically solve your struggle with lust and fornication. Perhaps you've finally found someone who checks all your boxes and you're terrified of letting them slip away.

Listen, if you're getting married for any reason other than to honor God and build a life with someone who shares your kingdom vision, you're setting yourself up for disappointment.

Marriage isn't a band-aid for your insecurities or a solution to your loneliness.

It's a sacred union that requires sacrifice, selflessness, and a whole lot of dying to self. Take some more time to fast and pray, to reevaluate your sense of self-worth, your true motivations, and your relationship with God. Until you're fully grounded in who you are in Christ, you're not ready to take this leap.

Marriage: A Sacred Covenant

Marriage is a sacred bond, meant to mirror the loving relationship between God and His church. It requires constant selflessness and sacrifice, as well as a strong foundation in faith. When you say "I do," you're not just joining your lives together—you're embarking on a journey of selflessness, sacrifice, and daily choosing to put your spouse's needs above your own.

I've been pretty clear about how crucial it is that the person you're considering spending forever with is saved and Spirit-filled. But let me tell you, even if you're both sold out for Jesus, your marriage isn't going to be perfect, or even anything remotely close to it. Regardless of how saved you both are, the ultimate reality the two of you must face is that you are marrying a sinner. There will be days when your spouse, despite his or her love for God and for you, will disappoint you, anger you, frustrate you, and yes, even hurt you—sometimes in small ways, other times in earth-shattering ways.

If you want your marriage to go the distance, your commitment to your spouse needs to be rooted in something far deeper than warm, fuzzy feelings. It has to be anchored in the unshakable conviction that God Himself is the center, the very foundation of your relationship. At this point in your dating journey, your primary focus should be on discerning whether this relationship aligns with God's will for your life.

Here's the raw truth—marriage will stretch your faith and your character like nothing else. Your spouse's imperfections (and your own) will test your spirit in ways you never imagined. If your relationship with God isn't the driving force behind your union, if your personal happiness and agenda take precedence over honoring the covenant you've made, you'll be tempted to bail when the going gets tough.

But walking away is not part of God's design for marriage. If this sacred bond is meant to reflect Christ's love for the church, then breaking your vows would imply that God's love for us is just as fickle. And we know that's not the case. Barring certain extreme circumstances, "I've fallen out of love," "This isn't what I expected," and "It's just too hard" are not valid reasons to jump ship. Marriage is a lifelong commitment.

When you shift your focus from your partner to God, marriage takes on a whole new weight. It becomes a profound opportunity to deepen your relationship with Him as you love and serve your spouse.

Will it be easy? Maybe. Will it be worth it? Absolutely. As you witness firsthand the relentless, unconditional love of Christ through the daily experience of marriage, you'll discover a new level of intimacy with God.

So, before you take this sacred leap, ask yourself—are you truly ready to lay down your life for this person? Are you firmly rooted in your identity in Christ? If you can't say "yes" with full confidence, it doesn't mean you have to end things. It simply means you need to slow down, gain some perspective, and make sure the person is worth the serious sacrifices you will ultimately make. At the end of the day, marriage is so much more than a feeling—it's a sacred calling to love as Christ loves His bride.

Engage Or Disengage

Let's be real—getting saved is easy. Jesus did all the heavy lifting on the cross. But actually living out this Christian life? That's a whole different ballgame. We'd all be perfect Christians if it wasn't for these bodies of ours messing with our spirit man, wouldn't we? The apostle Paul wasn't shy about admitting that his flesh was a constant battleground in Romans 7, and if he had to wrestle, you better believe we do too. In the realm of dating, nowhere is this struggle more pronounced.

So, when it comes to Christian dating, there comes a point where you have to make a decision: are you and your significant other headed towards engagement or not? Let me repeat myself—Christians should only be dating with one goal in mind: marriage. We're not in this for flings or playing the field. Messing around in the dating scene will only lead you straight into a minefield of premarital sex and a bunch of drama, from heartache to herpes. Trust me, you don't want to add any more bodies to your count.

If you're not absolutely blown away after the first date, don't bother with a second. I said this earlier in the book, but in case you forgot, the moment you realize this person isn't the one, cut things off ASAP. I'll say it louder for the people in the back: CHRISTIANS. DATE. TO. GET. MARRIED. End of story.

Every Sunday, my wife and I brace ourselves for the onslaught of ladies pouring out their hearts about the latest man they're seeing. So many of you reading this can probably relate—you're madly in love with some brother, but something in your spirit just isn't sitting right. You may have even already crossed physical boundaries with him. If you have, because of that soul tie forged between the sheets, you may be mistaking lust for love.

Here's the hard truth: Most of these men you're dating or sleeping with don't have the first clue about how to truly love a woman. Chances are, they've never had a godly role model demonstrating what it means to treat a woman with respect, honor, and chivalry.

If your daddy didn't model biblical love for your mama, if your uncles and cousins were just using women, if your church didn't teach you how to truly lead a household, how is a brother supposed to know how to do it right?

Single Moms, Take Note

Single mothers, please think about this. It may help you to understand (not excuse) your child/children's father(s) if they are not fulfilling their parental responsibilities. In many cases they don't know how to be good fathers because they've never seen it done right. Additionally, ask yourself why you chose to sleep with someone who had proved nothing, and made no godly commitments to be your husband or your children's father.

Women Love Hard, But Sometimes Too Hard

Y'all know how it is when a woman loves a man—she loves hard, no holding back. Her mom, her sister, and her riders can all tell her he is not the one, but tragically, she's gonna love him anyway until the damage is done.

Reflecting On Past Relationships

Ladies, think back to a man from your past who you knew wasn't the one, but you loved him anyway. As you look back, try to pinpoint exactly what it was that you loved about him. Here are a few questions to ask yourself:

- Did he invest in your spiritual growth by praying with you and studying God's Word together?

- Did he put your emotional, physical, and financial wellbeing above his own?

- Did he respect you enough to keep it zipped until the honeymoon? If you did have sex, did he genuinely repent and ask forgiveness from both God and you for not honoring your temple?

- Single moms, are your children better off spiritually, financially, mentally, and emotionally because of your relationship with him?

If you're honest, most times all you got was some good lovin' (which was straight sin!) and maybe good conversation. Besides the life lessons about dating a fool, you didn't get much else. Those of you with children might argue that at least he gave you a wonderful child, although you must realize that any man with healthy sperm could have done that for you. It wasn't God's will for you to get pregnant before you got married; He just loved you enough to bless you through it all.

Hear me loud and clear: lust takes, but love gives. If a man doesn't know Christ, how can he possibly love you the way you deserve? And even if he is saved, that doesn't automatically make him husband material. You can be saved and still be crazy; you can love Jesus and still be a hot mess. The brutal reality is that most men are utterly clueless about what a woman truly needs from them.

Take responsibility for the choices you've made concerning men. This includes the one you're dating now or will date in the future. Use the rules in this book to make good, solid choices in your current or next relationship. Either God sent him or He didn't. The quicker you find out the better. This means you'll endure less unnecessary drama.

So, what's a woman to do? Set the standard. Demand what you need. Don't settle for less than God's best for you. If the man you're with isn't stepping up to the plate, it might be time to reevaluate things.

The Ten "Demand-Ments" For All The Single Ladies

In Exodus 20, God gave His people Ten Commandments through His main man Moses. In a previous edition of this book, I took the liberty of drafting what I call the Ten "Demand-ments." As saved, single women, you must demand certain things from yourself and any man you seriously date. I understand that before my *Ten Rules* series, the word Demand-ments didn't exist, but it does now.

1. Demand yourself to love and trust God more than any man.

2. Demand yourself to pray, as well as read your Bible consistently.

3. Demand yourself to desire the filling of the Holy Spirit more than sex.

4. Demand yourself to go to a teaching church weekly and be active in the ministry you are called to.

5. Demand that any man who approaches you knows or is willing to get to know Jesus in an intimate way.

6. Demand that any man you date honors the God in you and treats you like a kingdom woman at all times.

7. Demand yourself to never allow any man to hit you and still have you.

8. Demand that any man you're considering marrying get as healthy as possible in every way before you marry him.

9. Demand of yourself that you never settle for any man that God did not send.

10. Demand that from this moment on, no man will ever have sex with you unless he's your husband.

Demanding The Best From Yourself

I know you can't literally demand an adult to do anything, but you can demand what they must do if they want to be with you. And you've got to demand certain things from yourself too. I love the way the Bible puts it in 1 Corinthians 9:26 (NLT): "I discipline my body like an athlete, training it to do what it should." Paul is saying in essence to put a demand on yourself to do what's right. I don't let my body run me, rather I allow the God in me, to run my body.

More Than A Pretty Face

For all the sexy girls lacking spiritual substance, here's a word from 1 Timothy 4:7-8 (NRSV): "Train yourself in godliness, for, while physical training is of some value, godliness is valuable in every way, holding promise for both the present life and the life to come."

Allow me to modernize, contemporize, and Vernon-ize this piece of the Bible. Paul is saying that to have a beautiful figure because you work out is great, but what good is it to have a sexy shape and still be sad? A great job but no joy? To be popular but still have no peace? Good habits but a bad heart? Nice clothes but ugly character? A master's degree but still masturbating? You can demand from yourself, with the power of God, to be the woman He has predestined you to become. Don't settle for less than the man He wants you have. Don't settle for being less than the kingdom woman He has called you to be.

All My Dogs

I'm sure by now you've noticed that I'm not the average pastor and this is not the average spiritual book on dating. In a sense, I write the way I preach. My approach, from the page to the stage, is raw, unfiltered, and unapologetically honest—it's style and substance.

If you ever find yourself in Cleveland, I invite you to experience The Word Church firsthand. You'll quickly see what sets us apart, not just in our message, but in our congregation's makeup. Unlike the norm, where you might find a sea of women filling the seats, our services attract thousands of men.

This wasn't by accident. Years ago, I made a conscious decision to cultivate a community that challenges the status quo. The truth is, in most churches, women make up the majority of the congregation, supporting the ministry in every possible way. As a result, many pastors and churches cater their messages and programs to what women want to see and hear. The same goes for Christian authors—they know women are more likely to buy their books, so they write with a female audience in mind. But my prayer is that this section, in particular, will reach the ears (and hearts) of some genuine single brothers who are hungry to become the kingdom men God has called them to be.

Now, you might be wondering about the title of this section, "All My Dogs." No, it's not a mistake. Even as a pastor, husband, father (and Alpha), I've still got some "dog" in me. I'm a red-blooded heterosexual man who loves to look at a beautiful woman with a bad body. Getting saved and filled with the Holy Spirit didn't change that. Men are visual creatures, plain and simple.

What's With The "Dog" Talk?

Now, let me break it down for the super spiritual folks who might be clutching their pearls right now. For years, I've listened to the women in my family vent about the trifling "dogs" who did them wrong, all while carrying their babies. I was honestly curious about this comparison of men and dogs.

It didn't take long to connect the dots. Women call men dogs because, like a dog in heat, most men will jump at the chance to sleep with any attractive female who crosses their path. As much as it pains me to admit it, I have to agree. The majority of men, myself included, would love to get with any woman who has the face and body that turns us on.

Here's what most women fail to realize: there are two types of dogs—trained and untrained. The untrained ones? We call those mutts. So, what's the difference? Glad you asked. A trained dog wants the same thing as an untrained one. The only difference is, one has a Master, and the other doesn't. The only thing that sets me apart from the average single man reading this book is that I fear and submit to my Master, Jesus Christ.

Stay On The Porch

Picture this: Someone's walking their female dog down the street and they pass by a house with a male dog sitting on the porch. That trained male dog wants to do the same thing a wild, untrained dog would do - jump off that porch and get it on with the female dog right then and there. But as soon as he looks like he's about to make a move or starts making that sound dogs make when they're ready to mate, his owner drops one word that shuts it all down: "Stay!" No matter how badly he wants it, when his owner says, "Stay, Boy!" it's enough to keep him on the porch.

Every single brother reading this needs to understand that he can't control his flesh on his own. He can't love a woman right without a power greater than himself. 1 John 4:4 (NASB) says, "...greater is He who is in you than he who is in the world." God is our Master. He demands that we honor the women in our lives in every way. So, when God tells us to "stay on the porch," that's exactly what we've got to do.

Training Day

Years ago, I preached this message called "Training Day" specifically for my black brothers, but really it applies to all men. I made the case that most men haven't been equipped with the tools to be godly husbands and fathers. I've been shouting it from the rooftops for years: You don't just wake up one day and magically become an incredible husband and dad. Sex? That's natural. But marriage and fatherhood? Those require training.

No one needs to teach you how to get busy in the bedroom; God designed it so we'd know what to do. But He also designed a system where your own father is supposed to model real love and respect for your mother, so you'd naturally repeat that behavior in your own household. How many of us can really say we had this example growing up?

Leaving A Trail Of Wounded Women

One reason I wrote this book is because I'm convinced most single men don't really know how to properly date and honor a woman. Most haven't learned how to stay celibate till marriage, let alone keep their virginity. In today's culture, the very idea of waiting until your wedding night to have sex is met with laughter and disbelief.

As a result, too many single brothers have been leaving a trail of wounded women behind them for years. I can't even count the number of men, even in my own church, who've confessed to me that they can't remember the names of all the women they've taken to bed. That's crazy! Somehow, they've gone through life with no one ever telling them that men should only sleep with their wives. Maybe no one ever made it clear that they should only get one woman pregnant, have all their children with that woman, and make sure that woman is their wife.

Protecting The Hearts Of Women

As I said previously, women tend to love harder than men. Some immature men take advantage of this. If a woman is over the age of twenty-five, there's a good chance she's had at least one child who needs and deserves their father, but can't have him, even though every child deserves a quality relationship with their dad. On top of that, the horrible reality is that many women, even in my own church, have been molested by some sick individual, robbing them of their innocence. The last thing these women need is more pain inflicted by careless men.

Make up your mind right now that you will honor, in every way, the woman you are currently dating or will date in the future. I'm blessed to have three beautiful sisters, two daughters, and a granddaughter that I would kill a man over! (I'm only half kidding).

I keep it simple. I treat my Victory the way I would want any man to treat my sisters and my daughters. I truly believe that God has thousands of brothers reading this book who don't even go to church, and I've got a feeling that He wants to use you to be a blessing to a woman. That's right—a blessing! My wife is blessed because she met me. I'm not just talking financially or mentally, but most importantly, spiritually.

Be A Giver, Not Just A Taker

I don't care what kind of baggage you're carrying or what your past looks like. There is a woman out there that you are meant to be a blessing to. As men, we're not just in relationships to receive. We should be giving, too. And don't even stress about whether you'll get anything in return. Most women will give back to you tenfold what you pour into them. It's just the way they're built. So, fellas, make the choice to be selfless. Love your future wife the way Ephesians 5:25-33 (GW) lays it out:

25 Husbands, love your wives as Christ loved the church and gave his life for it. 26 He did this to make the church holy by cleansing it, washing it using water along with spoken words. 27 Then he could present it to himself as a glorious church, without any kind of stain or wrinkle—holy and without faults. 28 So husbands must love their wives as they love their own bodies. A man who loves his wife loves himself. 29 No one ever hated his own body. Instead, he feeds and takes care of it, as Christ takes care of the church. 30 We are parts of his body. 31 That's why a man will leave his father and mother and be united with his wife, and the two will be one. 32 This is a great mystery. (I'm talking about Christ's relationship to the church.) 33 But every husband must love his wife as he loves himself, and wives should respect their husbands.

Man Up And Make A Decision

I'm dead serious about this "engage or disengage" thing. At some point you've got to answer this question as a man - is this woman God's wife for you? Do you love her enough to put a ring on it? Are you willing to do whatever it takes to be the man she deserves? The man God has called you to be?

If she's not the one, do the right thing and let her go. Don't string her along. It's better to walk away without ever having touched her or made empty promises but even if you have, if she's not wife material, cut ties cleanly and quickly. The longer you drag it out, the more she'll expect from you—and unmet expectations are a breeding ground for heartbreak.

That's why it infuriates me when I see men toying with women who were doing just fine before they came along. More often than not, she was living for the Lord, staying pure, and handling her business. She wasn't thirsty for a man; she was chasing after God's purpose for her life. But then some smooth-talking brother slides into her DMs, and because she's human and craves love just like the rest of us, she falls for him (usually way too fast). Make the decision today that you will never be *that* guy again.

If you've been dating a woman for a year, or two max, it's time to engage or disengage.

When You Know, You Know

On the flip side, if you've searched your heart and you know beyond a shadow of a doubt that she's the one, it's time to get down on one knee and lock it down. Don't waste another second. When you put a ring on it, you're making a public declaration that she's spoken for and so are you. No more flirtatious comments on other women's posts. No more wandering eyes. You're a one-woman man now. It's the biblical way. It's the right way. So man up, get your act together, and treat that woman like the queen she is.

RULE 10
DON'T HAVE SEX

"What we wait for speaks volumes about what we value." -*Dr. R. A. Vernon*

Keeping It Clean In A Dirty Dating Scene

In this final chapter, we confront the most challenging aspect of Christian dating—maintaining purity in a world that often doesn't. Some of you might be thinking, "Pastor, you've been saying this the whole book!" You're right, I have, but that's because it's just that important. The scriptures haven't changed, and neither has my position. So, as we delve deeper into this final admonition, let's bring to light not just the commandment, but the heart and soul behind it.

Our culture is oversexed and under-loved. Everywhere you look, sex is being sold. But your body is not a commodity, and your heart is not for rent.

Wait For It...

The patience you exhibit in waiting for the right time, the right person, and the right conditions, speaks volumes to the world about your commitment to God and yourself. It's not merely about choosing to abstain; it's why you make the choice. This decision to honor God with your body before marriage tells a powerful story of faith, self-respect, and self-mastery.

The reality is, God designed sex to be amazing—a mind-blowing experience that unites a husband and wife together in a celebration of love that is as deeply spiritual as it is delightfully physical. It's meant to be the pinnacle experience of intimacy, where the divine gift of pleasure meets the human expression of love in a covenant marriage relationship.

Peep this quote from C.S. Lewis, where he poignantly captures the meaning of sex within covenant, and the fundamental problem of sexual activity outside of it:

> The monstrosity of sexual intercourse outside marriage is that those who indulge in it are trying to isolate one kind of union (the sexual) from all the other kinds of union which were intended to go along with it and make up the total union. The Christian attitude does not mean that there is anything wrong about sexual pleasure, any more than about the pleasure of eating. It means that you must not isolate that pleasure and try to get it by itself, any more than you ought to try to get the pleasures of taste without swallowing and digesting, by chewing things and spitting them out again. – *Mere Christianity*

Lewis is cutting straight to the heart of the matter. The reason premarital sex is such a perversion is because it takes this intense physical union meant to be combined with the spiritual, mental, emotional and covenantal unions, and distorts it into just a physical act disconnected from its deeper purpose and power. Some people want the pleasure without the promise, which leads to dissonance, disharmony, and desecration, resulting in an erosion of true intimacy.

Let Me Set Your Sexpectations: The Fallacy Of Fragmented Fulfillment

Think about it this way: God created sex to be a powerful bonding agent, a way for a husband and wife to express their complete unity and devotion to one another. It's meant to be a physical manifestation of the "one flesh" relationship described in Genesis 2:24. When we experience sexual pleasure apart from this context, we're saying, "I want the thrill of the moment without the sacrifice of a lifetime."

As Lewis explains, this approach is fundamentally flawed. He compares it to trying to enjoy the taste of food without actually swallowing and digesting it. Can you imagine chewing up some succulent steak and then spitting it out? That's nasty, right? But that's essentially what we're doing when we try to experience the pleasure of sex without the full covenant commitment. Just as our bodies were designed to receive nourishment through the full process of eating, our souls were designed to experience sexual intimacy within the full context of the marriage covenant.

> **God designed sex to be one of the most exquisite, transcendent experiences we could ever have—a foretaste of heaven's joy right here on earth.**

This is what Lewis means when says that the Christian view isn't that sexual enjoyment itself is wrong, just like there's nothing wrong with enjoying the taste of food. The key is that it must be enjoyed within the proper boundaries, as part of the "total union" of marriage. When we honor God's design, we open ourselves up to a depth of intimacy, trust, and joy that the world's version of sex can never provide.

From Good To Great: The Progression Of Intimacy In Marriage

Sex is one of God's greatest gifts to humankind. Fortunately for my wife and me, with each passing year, we enjoy an even deeper sexual connection. God (and Peloton!) makes her more attractive to me each year we stay married. We are experiencing a much greater level of sexual enjoyment in our fifties than we did in our twenties. I'm sure my adult kids who are single and reading this are about to throw up right now, but it's my story and I'm sticking to it.

Some of you are thinking, why is he talking to singles about great sex in the don't-have-sex part of the book? I'm glad you asked! When is the last time you heard a married man whose wife had birthed five kids —six if you include the one we lost because he came prematurely—talk about how much he loves her and loves making love to her?

Dismantling The Devil's Distortions Of Sex

There's so much misinformation and disinformation circulating in culture that we have to talk about sex in its proper context—marriage—to counter the harmful messages that society often sends our way. We are led to believe by movies, media, and the internet, that the epitome of sexual experience is found in the restless pursuit of variety, in constantly seeking new partners and experiences. These are all lies.

The devil knows the power of sex in marriage, the connection it sustains between man and woman, making them one flesh. He has no original ideas, so he takes God's divine designs and tries to twist them. God's original intention in Genesis 2 was for a man and woman to connect in marriage, be fruitful, and multiply. Well, there is only one way to do that, right? The only people I hear bragging on great sex are the very people who should not be having it. Singles!

If you believe in God and the Bible, then you have to stop playing with this sex thing. If you're not married, sex is disgusting, damaging, dangerous, deadly, devastating, depressing, depleting, deluding, diluted, and dumb! Whenever you do something that can destroy your body and your soul just because it makes you feel good for an hour (or a minute depending on the person you're being dumb with) sounds crazy to me.

Don't Give It Away

I promised myself that I was going to write a book that singles could feel in their soul—a book that you could recommend to every unmarried person you know, even those who don't go to church. For that to be a reality, I knew I had to be authentic and straightforward about the real struggles that singles face.

The truth is, the average single reading this has likely already had sex. Let's be real, most of you are sleeping with somebody right now. Maybe not every day, or even every month, but any time outside of marriage is too much. I'm under no illusion that this book is being read exclusively by virgins. To you rare singles that have made it by His grace to your 18th birthday and are still pure, keep this same energy until you get married. Don't give away the precious gift of your virginity.

First Times And Lost Times

If you ask the average single person if they are proud of losing their virginity, most will confess that they are not. The majority of people didn't truly enjoy their first sexual experience, and tragically, many no longer even remember the person with whom they shared what was meant to be one of the most significant moments of their lives.

I am going to make every effort to persuade dating couples to wait until their honeymoon to engage in any form of sexual pleasure with each other. Even if you've had multiple sexual partners in the past, God will bless your current relationship if you choose to honor Him moving forward. Before I continue, I want to take a moment to address the young singles, including preteens, who have had the perseverance to wait and maintain their sexual purity. The following section is especially for you.

Virgin Territory: Guarding Your Most Precious Gift

God, in His infinite wisdom, designed human sexuality with a physical sign of a woman's virginity. He placed a "do not open until marriage" seal upon her, known as the hymen. This membrane, located at the opening of the vagina, is typically not broken except through sexual intercourse. While the use of certain feminine hygiene products can sometimes cause the hymen to break before intercourse, it remains a natural, physical symbol that a woman is to remain "unopened" until the right time.

When a woman has sex for the first time and her hymen is broken, she often bleeds onto her partner's penis. This blood is traditionally believed to represent a covenant—a promise that the man who breaks it is the first and will be the last man she will ever share this intimate act with, barring death.

White Dress, White Sheets: The Ultimate Wedding Night

As a virgin, you have a once-in-a-lifetime opportunity to offer your spouse something that every non-virgin reading this wishes they could

—the gift of your pure, untouched self! I've officiated more weddings than I can remember. To this day, I have never married two virgins.

Can you imagine being that groom, looking fresh in your tux, watching your beautiful, sanctified, sexy fiancée walking down the aisle toward you? She's never been touched, and neither have you. As you're repeating your vows, you're looking into her beautiful eyes and thinking very spiritual thoughts like, "I'M GOING TO KILL THAT TONIGHT!" Seriously folks, or should I say *spiritually* folks, virginity is a precious thing. Don't give it away!

When physical virginity is lost, it is lost forever, but the virginity of the heart can be restored through the power of the Holy Spirit. Even if you can't regain your physical virginity, you can repent of your sins—sexual and otherwise—and God will give you a clean heart, a new heart, a childlike heart, a virginal heart. In God's eyes, it will be as if you had never sinned or done anything wrong.

Lovers, Locusts, And The Lord: A Prayer For Reclaimed Purity

Just as Paul desired to present the Corinthians as pure virgins to Christ (2 Corinthians 11), I too want to present you as a spotless bride to our Bridegroom, Jesus Christ. So, let's pray:

> Heavenly Father,
>
> I realize tonight that through my own sinful desires, the temptations of this world, and the tricks of the devil himself, I have lost my virginity. I've allowed other people and things to penetrate my life, forfeiting my purity and depriving my future spouse of an untouched body and soul.
>
> I've willfully pursued other lovers at times, and I acknowledge how sinful my attitudes and actions have

been. I truly repent of those attitudes and sins. I am so sorry for the relational pain I've caused others and You.

I accept Your forgiveness right now!

I renounce any and all illegitimate suitors to my body and heart, and wholeheartedly reserve myself for You and the one person You have for me. Help me to walk in the new life that the blood of Jesus provides. In Jesus' name, Amen.

THE STORY THAT KEEPS ON GIVING

I want to close this book with a powerful story that I believe will inspire you. If you've read the previous editions of this book, then you're already familiar with it. But if you know the power of stories, you understand how they allow us to see things in ways that objective facts and strong opinions don't. That's why I keep sharing this particular story, because to this day, it remains one of the most striking examples of dating and getting married the right way that I have ever witnessed.

Some years ago, this young brother Antonio at our church, who was engaged to a sister named Rachael, came to my office. He told me he made a bold decision about their engagement - not only was he committed to not having sex with Rachael before the wedding night, but he wasn't gonna kiss her or even hold her hand until they met at the altar.

I was stunned. At the time, it seemed so radical, so counter-cultural, that I hardly knew how to respond. I had never encountered anyone who had attempted such a thing, and a part of me wondered if it was even possible. Yet, as I looked into Antonio's eyes, I saw a man who was sincere in his conviction. I knew I couldn't stand in the way of such devotion. So, with a mixture of awe and apprehension, I simply said, "Okay," and left it at that.

Week after week, I would check in with Antonio, fully expecting him to admit that he had caved to temptation. "Pastor, no, I haven't kissed her," he'd say, and each time, my respect for them grew. As their big day got closer, I found myself increasingly invested. Now, I was rooting for them, caught up in the suspense of their journey.

By the time their wedding day arrived, Antonio was over the moon with anticipation. They had made it - without a single kiss or any kind of sexual contact! To add even more beauty and meaning, Rachael and Antonio had come up with this poignant symbolic idea for their ceremony that I'd never seen before. They decided that Rachael would walk down the aisle first, and then Antonio would come out and follow in her footsteps to meet her at the altar. They wanted to depict Christ the Bridegroom coming for His bride, the Church in the most vivid way possible.

Rachael was a breathtaking bride, and from our vantage point in my office, Antonio and I watched as she gracefully made her way down the aisle through a small opening in the door. Just as she reached the altar, Antonio dashed out of another door and ran around the building so that he could literally follow in her footsteps and meet her at the end of the aisle, in front of the altar.

He strolled down the walkway, as giddy and joyful as any man could be. They soon began repeating their vows, and the moment came when I spoke the words that the two of them couldn't wait to hear: "By the power vested in me by the state of Ohio and the authority of Jesus Christ, our Lord and Savior, I now pronounce you husband and wife. You may kiss your bride."

A Kiss That Shook The Heavens

The moment Antonio lifted Rachael's veil to seal their union with a kiss, the presence of God descended upon that place and enveloped us all. I had never felt anything so pure and powerful during a wedding, and I still haven't to this day. The anointing was so thick and overwhelming it took everything in me to remain standing.

This, my friends, is what it means to do it right. Antonio and Rachael had made it to their wedding day without crossing a single physical or spiritual boundary, and the blessings that flowed from their obedience were undeniable. Today, nearly twenty years later, they are still happily married with two boys, with thriving careers and a successful business.

Regardless of what they had done in their past, their relationship was a virgin relationship. They were virgins in Christ. They had never experienced sexual intimacy with one another before their wedding night and had never even felt each other's lips before I pronounced them husband and wife.

The God Of Endless Chances

Their story is a testament to the truth that no matter your past, no matter how many mistakes you've made or how far you think you've fallen, God is a God of redemption. He is a God of second, third, and countless chances. When you choose to honor Him with your body, your heart, and your relationships, He will guide you into a relationship that glorifies Him. He will prove Himself faithful; His plans are always for your good.

So, I challenge you today, as you close this book and step into the next chapter of your life, to make a decision. Decide that regardless of what you've done before, you will do the next relationship right. Decide to abstain from sex—until you stand before God and your loved ones, pledging your life and love to the one He has chosen for you.

Imagine sitting down with your kids one day and telling them, "Your mom and I? We did it God's way," knowing that because you chose to honor God with your body and your relationship, you just might save your son or daughter years of heartache and pain from making the same mistakes you did. Imagine being that couple that everyone looks at and says, "There's something different about them."

Remember, God is not looking for perfection. He knows you're human. He knows you're going to mess up. What He's looking for is a heart that says, "God, I'm all in. I trust you. I want to do things your way, even when it's hard." When you give Him that kind of commitment, watch out! There's no telling what kind of crazy, amazing, inconceivable blessings He's going to pour out on you. There's no limit to what He can and will do in and through you when you're willing to honor him no matter what.

Delayed Gratification: The Compounding Interest Of Obedience

All those nights you spent praying instead of straying, every date where you chose conversation over compromise, every step taken in faith and not in haste, will be rewarded, not in-kind, but manifold.

That's what you're fighting for. That's what you're holding out for. And trust me, when you're standing there on your wedding day, looking into the eyes of the one God created just for you, you'll know beyond a shadow of a doubt that it was all worth it.

The choice is yours - will you settle for temporary pleasures that leave you empty and unsatisfied? Or will you go all in with God, trusting Him with every area of your life, including your relationships?

I'm here to tell you that steadfast obedience doesn't just bring biblical promises to life - it unlocks a depth of intimacy with your Creator that makes anything the world has to offer look like dirt.

As Antonio and Rachael's story so powerfully illustrates, the true reward of pursuing purity and trusting God with your relationships is not found in a perfect earthly love story, but in the unshakable knowledge that you are walking in agreement with your Heavenly Father's best laid plans for you.

You're More Than Your Relationship Status

By choosing to glorify God with your physical, emotional, and relational choices, you are making a powerful statement about who you are in Christ. By making this choice, you are announcing to the world that you belong to Him, that your worth is rooted in His love for you, and that your purpose is to live in a way that brings honor and praise to His name

And here's the beautiful truth: Whether God's plan for you includes marriage or not, His love for you remains constant, His presence with you remains unwavering, and His purpose for your life remains unshakable.

Your value, your joy, and your fulfillment are not contingent upon your relationship status. They are rooted in the unchanging reality of who you are in Christ—beloved, chosen, and called to a life of significance and impact.

So, as you close this book and step into the next chapter of your journey, I challenge you to fix your eyes not on an earthly romance, but on the Author of your story. Trust Him with your desires, your dreams, and your deepest longings, knowing that He is able to do immeasurably more than you could ever ask or imagine.

Pursue purity, not as a means to an end, but as an act of worship, a daily choice to honor the God who created you, redeemed you, and called you His own. Surround yourself with a community of believers who will encourage you, support you, and hold you accountable to living a life that reflects Christ's love and holiness.

As you walk this path of obedience, know that your story and your faithfulness have the power to impact countless lives. Whether through your singleness or your marriage, your life can be living testimony of God's grace and goodness.

Squad Goals: Your Heavenly Hype Team

So, take heart, my friend. I know I've said this elsewhere, but as I close, it bears repeating again. You are not alone on this journey. You have a Heavenly Father who loves you, a Savior who redeems you, and a Holy Spirit who empowers you. You have a cloud of witnesses cheering you on, a community of believers standing with you, and a world waiting to be impacted by your story.

Trust that as you seek Him first, as you delight yourself in Him, He will give you the desires of your heart—not necessarily in the way you expect, but always in the way that brings Him the most glory and does you the most good.

This is your moment. This is your invitation. Will you trust Him? Will you say yes to His best for your life, regardless of your relationship status?

I believe you will. I believe you're ready. Embrace the adventure of living each day in the fullness of His presence, the certainty of His love, and the joy of His purpose for your life. I can't wait to see the amazing story He writes with your life.

NOTES

[1] Unmarried and Single Americans Week: September 17-23, 2023 (census.gov)

[2] Americans' Views on Dating and Relationships | Pew Research Center

[3] Ibid.

[4] Online Dating Statistics in 2023: Trends & Surprising Insights - Hack Spirit

[5] Dating and relationships: Key findings on views and experiences in the US | Pew Research Center; From Swiping to Sexting: The Enduring Gender Divide in American Dating and Relationships - The Survey Center on American Life (americansurveycenter.org)

[6] Ibid.

[7] Online dating is the most popular way couples meet | Stanford News; https://hackspirit.com/online-dating-statistics/

[8] Situationships, breadcrumbing, the ick: Viral dating terms, explained (usatoday.com)

[9] What Self-Awareness Really Is (and How to Cultivate It) (hbr.org)

[10] https://www.brides.com/story/modern-arranged-marriages

Experience is not always the best teacher. It is, however, the hardest teacher.

[11] https://www.census.gov/library/stories/2023/09/unmarried-women-men.html

[12] Cloud, Henry. Necessary Endings: The Employees, Businesses, and Relationships That All of Us Have to Give Up in Order to Move Forward. HarperBusiness, 2011